NONEXISTENT OBJECTS IN BUDDHIST PHILOSOPHY

ALSO AVAILABLE FROM BLOOMSBURY

Chinese and Buddhist Philosophy in Early Twentieth-Century German Thought, by Eric S. Nelson

Confucian Ethics in Western Discourse, by Wai-ying Wong

Cultivating a Good Life in Early Chinese and Ancient Greek Philosophy, edited by Karyn Lai, Rick Benitez and Hyun Jin Kim

Natural and Artifactual Objects in Contemporary Metaphysics, edited by Richard Davies

Realisms Interlinked, by Arindam Chakrabarti

NONEXISTENT OBJECTS IN BUDDHIST PHILOSOPHY

On Knowing What There is Not

ZHIHUA YAO

BLOOMSBURY ACADEMIC
LONDON • NEW YORK • OXFORD • NEW DELHI • SYDNEY

BLOOMSBURY ACADEMIC
Bloomsbury Publishing Plc
50 Bedford Square, London, WC1B 3DP, UK
1385 Broadway, New York, NY 10018, USA
29 Earlsfort Terrace, Dublin 2, Ireland

BLOOMSBURY, BLOOMSBURY ACADEMIC and the Diana logo are trademarks of Bloomsbury Publishing Plc

First published in Great Britain 2020
This paperback edition published in 2021

Cover design: Louise Dugdale
Cover image: Katrin Ray Shumakov / Getty images

A catalogue record for this book is available from the British Library.

A catalog record for this book is available from the Library of Congress.

ISBN: HB: 978-1-3501-2147-8
PB: 978-1-3502-7310-8
ePDF: 978-1-3501-2148-5
eBook: 978-1-3501-2149-2

Typeset by Newgen KnowledgeWorks Pvt. Ltd., Chennai, India

CONTENTS

Acknowledgments viii

Introduction 1

I.1 Cognition of Nonexistent Objects 1

I.2 Speaking about Nonexistent Objects 6

I.3 Types of Nothing 8

PART ONE Cognition of Nonexistent Objects: A Historical Development 11

1 Mahāsāṃghika 13

1.1 Latent Defilements without Objects 13

1.2 Awareness without Objects 19

1.3 Consciousness of the Past and the Future 23

1.4 Three Arguments 26

2 Dārṣṭāntika 29

2.1 Objects of Conjunction and Feeling 29

2.2 Illusions 32

2.3 Negative Expressions 36

2.4 Meditation of Nonexistent Objects 37

2.5 Four Arguments 44

3 Yogācāra 47

3.1 "Mental Consciousness Takes Nonexistents as Objects" 47

3.2 The Past and the Future 49

3.3 Existents and Nonexistents 52
3.4 No-Self and Impermanence 55
3.5 Food and Drinks 59
3.6 Heretical Views 61
3.7 Five Arguments 63

4 Vasubandhu 65

4.1 Vaibhāṣika Arguments for the Existence of the Past and the Future 66
4.2 Conditions of Cognition 68
4.3 Speaking of the Past and the Future 72
4.4 Cognition of the Past and the Future 75
4.5 Ontological Status of the Past and the Future 79
4.6 Absolute Nonexistence 81
4.7 Doubts 83
4.8 Six Arguments 86

PART TWO Epistemological Approaches to Nonexistence 91

5 Non-cognition 93

5.1 A Third *Pramāṇa* 94
5.2 *Feiliang* 96
5.3 *Apramāṇatā (Apramāṇatva)* 99
5.4 Non-cognition and Nonexistence 102
5.5 Non-cognition as the Third *Pramāṇa* 106

6 Empty Terms 111

6.1 "Primordial Matter Does Not Exist" 112
6.2 The Method of Paraphrase 114
6.3 The Principle of Conceptual Subjects 117

6.4 Two Types of Negation 120

6.5 The Principle of Propositional Attitude 123

7 Negative Judgments 129

7.1 How is a Negative Judgment Possible? 129

7.2 Negation is Secondary 133

8 Typology of Nothing 141

8.1 Original Nothing 142

8.2 Nothing 147

8.3 Emptiness 149

8.4 Why is there Something Rather than Nothing? 153

Notes 157

References 175

Index 183

ACKNOWLEDGMENTS

I began working on some of the ideas advanced in this book more than a decade ago. Over the years, I have benefited from exchanging ideas with many colleagues and friends, especially Achim Bayer, Ven. Dhammajoti, Toru Funayama, Shoryu Katsura, Birgit Kellner, Gereon Kopf, Chen-kuo Lin, Dan Lusthaus, Andrew McGarrity, Bo Mou, Liangkang Ni, Graham Priest, Qingjie Wang, Guang Xing, and the late Lester Embree. This work was supported by the Academy of Korean Studies (KSPS) Grant funded by the Korean government (MOE) (AKS-2012-AAZ-2102). My special thanks to Jeson Woo for his encouragement.

Some chapters of the book appeared in their early versions as journal articles in *Journal of Indian Council of Philosophical Research* 25.3 (2008): 79–96 (Chapter 1), *Journal of Indian Philosophy* 37 (2009): 383–98 (Chapter 6), and *Comparative Philosophy* 1.1 (2010): 78–89 (Chapter 8). Some other chapters first appeared as book chapters in *Nothingness in Asian Philosophy* edited by Jeeloo Liu and Douglas Berger (Routledge 2014) 133–47 (Chapter 3), *Indian Epistemology and Metaphysics* edited by Joerg Tuske (Bloomsbury Academic 2017) 397–416 (Chapter 4), *Religion and Logic in Buddhist Philosophical Analysis* edited by Helmut Krasser et al. (Wien: Verlag der Österreichischen Akademie der Wissenschaften 2011) 477–90 (Chapter 5), and *Phenomenology 2005 Vol. I: Selected Essays from Asia* edited by Cheung Chan-fai and Yu Chung-chi (Bucharest: Zeta Books 2007) 731–46 (Chapter 7). I thank the editors and publishers for permission to include the revised version of these works in the current book. My thanks also go to two anonymous reviewers for their encouragements and constructive remarks, and to Colleen Coalter and Becky Holland of Bloomsbury for making the publication process smooth.

Introduction

I.1 Cognition of Nonexistent Objects

Ever since Leibniz, the fundamental question of metaphysics has been: "Why is there something rather than nothing?" But before we can start to ponder on this problem, we should have some sense of the meanings of "being" (or "what there is") and "nothing" (or "what there is not"). Philosophers throughout history have devoted themselves to these two subjects by developing the field of ontology. If, however, we are not satisfied with traditional speculative metaphysics, we could ask a more fundamental question, that is, "How do we know what there is or what there is not?" While the question "How do we know what there is?" makes perfect sense and has helped to plant the fruitful field of epistemology, the question "How do we know what there is not, or nonbeing?" encountered skepticism from the very beginning. A natural and even more fundamental question is: "Can we know what there is not?" or "How is it possible to know what there is not?" In other words, we need to ask whether we could possibly know nonbeing.

A group of Western and Asian philosophers answered "no" to this question. They denied the possibility of knowing nonbeing by claiming that "thought and being are the same" (Parmenides) or "whatever that is knowable (*jñeyatva*) is existence or being (*astitva*)" (Vaiśeṣikas, Sarvāstivāda Buddhists). This extreme view that expels nonbeing or nonexistence from the realms of knowledge and ontology has been influential in the history of Western and Eastern philosophy and developed into different varieties.

An apparent alternative answer to the question of whether we can know what there is not is "yes." A quick assertion to support this answer is that whatever that is knowable includes both being and nonbeing, hence thought equals being plus nonbeing. In this way, we have made knowability (*jñeyatva*), or potential intentional objects, a more fundamental ontological concept than being or nonbeing. On this view, we can know nonbeing, or what there is not, as well as we know being, or what there is. But the issue is how to prove this assertion. Meinong has famously justified the ontological status of nonbeing by distinguishing thus-being (*Sosein*) from being (*Sein*). According to him, one can meaningfully talk or know the thus-being or characteristics of a nonexistent object without committing oneself to the being or existence of this object.

Several Buddhist philosophical schools also attempted to prove this view of the knowability of nonexistents by developing various arguments against the extreme view of their main opponent, the Sarvāstivādins. The Sarvāstivāda Buddhists proposed their famous argument for the existence of the past and the future, which can be formulated as follows:

1 Whatever is knowable is existent.
2 The past and the future are knowable.
3 Therefore, the past and the future exist.

To support premise 1, the Sarvāstivādins refer to a theory of cognition commonly accepted by major Buddhist schools. That is, a cognition is possible with two conditions, a basis (i.e., sense) and an object (i.e., the knowable), and both act as generating conditions (*janaka-pratyaya*) of the cognition. Since a nonexistent cannot produce anything, it cannot be a generating condition of cognition and hence is not an object of cognition. Therefore, whatever is knowable or an object of cognition, it must be existent. There are some other arguments for the existence of the past and the future from metaphysical and soteriological grounds, but this epistemological argument is the most intriguing one, which has aroused much debate.

Other Buddhist schools (including Mahāsāṃghika, Yogācāras, and Sautrāntikas) do not accept the existence of the past and the future, so they have to find ways to refute this rather powerful argument. They do not dispute much on premise 2; instead they focus on refuting premise 1 by arguing that nonexistence is also knowable, hence the concept of the cognition of nonexistent objects. But how to prove this assertion? Similar to Meinong who distinguishes between thus-being and being, the Buddhists take a key step in distinguishing between generating condition (*janaka-pratyaya*) and condition in a quality of object (*ālambana-pratyaya*). An object is one of the two basic conditions for the arising of cognition, but it does not have to be its generating condition; instead, it can be a condition in the sense of object only. A nonexistent apparently cannot produce anything, so it cannot be a generating condition of cognition. But if this distinction holds, then a nonexistent can still be a condition of cognition in the quality of object, hence the cognition of nonexistent objects is established. This way, they have refuted premise 1, and, as a result, conclusion 3 is falsified.

As we see, both parties do not dispute the concept of generating condition. In fact, this is a basic definition of existence accepted by both sides. Though the Sarvāstivādins hold that all the three times exist, they still maintain that they exist in a different sense or degree. The present exists in the sense that it can exercise function or activity (*kāritra*) to produce certain effects, whereas all the three times exist in terms of their knowability (*jñeyatva*). Other Buddhist schools accept their definition of the present existence (at least on the conventional level) and further elaborate this definition in terms of causal power or causal efficacy (*arthakriyā*), which became a rather standard understanding of existence for late Indian Buddhists. A similar view is also found among some contemporary philosophers. For instance, Priest (2016: xxviii) holds that "to exist is to have the potential to interact causally."

This second aspect of the Sarvāstivāda definition of existence in terms of knowability is the same idea that is expressed in premise 1, which is also shared by the Vaiśeṣikas and the Greek philosopher Parmenides. But other Buddhist schools reject this definition. For them, a nonexistent can also be a knowable object. At this point, they distinguish two senses of condition. The past and the future can be conditions of cognition in the quality of object, but not in the sense of generating condition. Therefore, they conclude that the past and the future do *not* exist.

However, their commitment to the nonexistence of the past makes it especially difficult for them to explain some soteriological issues such as karmic retribution. A particular school—the Kāśyapīyas—holds instead that the past karmas that have not yet retributed still exist. Among contemporary philosophers, it is also a controversial issue whether the past and the future exist. Hence, many of them (e.g., Crane 2013: 16) tend to shy away from the past or the future in their discussions of nonexistence. In contrast, many Buddhist schools are committed to the nonexistence of the past and the future in their arguments for the cognition of nonexistent objects. Their denial of the existence of the past and the future could have been influenced by the popular fourfold classification of nonexistence among Indian philosophers. These include prior nonexistence (*prāgabhāva*), posterior nonexistence (*dhvaṃsa*), mutual nonexistence (*anyonyābhāva*), and absolute nonexistence (*atyantābhāva*). Among them, the first two types can be understood as the future and the past respectively.

Besides arguments from the past and the future, these schools also argue for the cognition of nonexistent objects from other types of nonexistence. They include absolute nonexistence (such as the son of a barren woman and a rabbit's horn), illusions, abstract universals, and some special meditative objects. Some arguments are also associated with negative expressions, cognitive doubts or errors, and emotional experiences. In Part I, I will analyze these arguments in detail with four chapters arranged in historical order: Mahāsāṃghika, Dārṣṭāntika, early Yogācāra, and Vasubandhu.

In the Buddhist Epistemological School represented by Dignāga and Dharmakīrti, we do not find explicit discussions on the concept of the cognition of nonexistent objects. Instead, they developed some new concepts to deal with the epistemological issues with regard to nonexistence, which is the focus of Chapters 5 and 7. I will begin with a study on Īśvarasena, who unfortunately left us no writings. Based on some indirect sources, we know that one of his main contributions was to propose an independent means of knowledge (*pramāṇa*) over and above perception (*pratyakṣa*) and inference (*anumāna*). This third means of knowledge is responsible for cognizing negative facts; it is called the mere absence of cognition (*upalabdhyabhāvamātra*), mere non-perception (*adarśanamātra*), or non-cognition (*apramāṇatā, apramāṇatva*).

Dharmakīrti, on the other hand, developed his elaborate theory of negative cognition or non-cognition (*anupalabdhi*) by arguing against his teacher Īśvarasena, the Naiyāyikas, and the Mīmāṃsaka Kumārila. First of all, he does not agree with the Naiyāyikas in reducing non-cognition to perception, nor with Īśvarasena and Kumārila in counting non-cognition as an independent means of knowledge. Instead, he includes non-cognition under inference and treats it as one of the three evidences (*hetu*) that ensure sound inferences. Therefore, he would take "negative judgment" to mean literally that "negation is judgment."

Second, to make non-cognition a valid inference, Dharmakīrti distinguishes between non-cognitions of perceptible and "imperceptible objects." The term "imperceptible objects" refers to supersensory or abstract objects, the non-cognition of which, according to him, cannot determine their nonexistence. For instance, from the non-cognition of ghosts one cannot conclude that ghosts do not exist. On the contrary, the absence of perceptible objects is proved if and only if they are not perceived when all the conditions for perception are fulfilled. Dharmakīrti limits himself to the discussion of the non-cognition of these perceptible objects, and only deals with negation of empirical objects or facts. This position has its advantages in avoiding issues involved with negative existential propositions.

Third, the non-cognition of perceptible objects, being an inference, is based on affirmative perceptions. According to Dharmakīrti, we have to know that there is nothing there through inference instead of simply through seeing or hearing. The fact that "there is no pottery on the table" is known through an inferential judgment that is based on the perception of the table instead of the pottery. In other words, the negation of the existence of pottery is an inferential judgment based on the normal perceptions of things other than pottery, for example, the table and so on.

I.2 Speaking about Nonexistent Objects

Besides the difficulties involving the *cognition* of nonexistent objects, there are also difficulties in speaking about nonexistents. Many contemporary philosophers are attracted by this issue as is evident in Russell's paradigm case of "the present king of France is bald." The Buddhists were also puzzled by the way of speaking about nonexistents, and they were particularly wrestling with such propositions as "*x* does not exist," known as singular existence-denials among contemporary philosophers (Chakrabarti 1997: 1ff). It may be false or nonsensical to say that "The present king of France is bald" or "The son of a barren women is tall," but statements like "The present king of France or the son of a barren women does not exist" make perfect sense and are certainly true. In fact, some of the foundational Buddhist doctrines such as no-self (*anātman*), impermanence (*anitya*), and emptiness (*śūnyatā*) can be rephrased into this type of proposition: "The self does not exist"; "A permanent entity does not exist"; "Intrinsic nature does not exist" (*niḥsvabhāvatā*). The subjects of these propositions are all considered as empty terms because, as stated in the propositions themselves, what they denote does not exist.

In Chapter 6, I classify the ways of dealing with the problem of empty terms in the Buddhist Epistemological School into four approaches: (1) the distinction of two types of negation; (2) the principle of propositional attitude; (3) the principle of conceptual subjects; and (4) the method of paraphrase. First of all, the distinction between two types of negation helps to justify such statement as "The self does not exist" or "A rabbit's horn does not exist." Both statements are involved with non-implicative negation (*prasajya-pratiṣedha*), which is different from implicative negation (*paryudāsa*), for example, "A rabbit's horn is not sharp." The Buddhist logical rule that distinguishes two types of negation allows empty subject terms in statements with non-implicative negation, but not in the ones with implicative negation. This explains why such statements as "A rabbit's horn does not exist" sound meaningful and true, but those like "A rabbit's horn is not sharp" are meaningless.

The Hindu opponents, however, may respond by saying: "We are not asking whether the self exists or not. Rather we are asking whether the self is different from the body." In the debating practice in ancient India, although it is required that the subject of an inferential statement be accepted by both the proponent and the opponent, there are cases when they do not commonly accept the subject of the statement. In the current case, the subject term "self" is accepted by the Hindu opponents, but not by the Buddhists. The Buddhist logicians would apply the principle of propositional attitude to require the opponents to add a presuppositional distinguisher in their question or statement. Their earlier question would be reformulated as follows: "Is the self *that we believe in* different from the body?" The presuppositional distinguisher indicates that they are imposing their wrong beliefs on the Buddhists and not really engaging in a serious dialogue.

The principle of conceptual subjects was popularly adopted by late Indian and Tibetan Buddhists to deal with the problem of empty subject terms. It is strictly speaking a more fundamental philosophical position that eliminates the problem of empty terms in its entirety and enables one to speak freely about such nonexistent entities as the self. For instance, the Buddhists, although denying the real existence of the self, can still say, "The self is permanent, so we do not accept it." In this case, the "self" is taken to be a concept that is not backed up by a real entity, and it is not involved in a logical fallacy when talking about its properties such as "permanence."

The method of paraphrase resembles Russell's theory of descriptions, which is the most important technically logical method to deal with empty terms among Western philosophers. Although it was underdeveloped in the Buddhist logical tradition, we still find some cases in which this method is applied to tackle the problem of empty terms.

I.3 Types of Nothing

Parmenides and the Sarvāstivādins expelled nonbeing from the realm of knowledge and forbade us to think or talk about it. But still there has been a long tradition of nay-sayings throughout the history of Western and Eastern philosophy. Are those philosophers talking about the same nonbeing or nothing? If not, how do their concepts of nothing differ from each other? Could there be different types of nothing? In the final chapter, I will address these questions.

Surveying the traditional classifications of nothing or nonbeing in the East and West have led me to develop a typology of nothing that consists of three main types: (1) privative nothing, commonly known as absence; (2) negative nothing, the altogether not or absolute nothing; and finally (3) original nothing, the nothing that is equivalent to being. I will test my threefold typology of nothing by comparing the similarities and differences between the concept of nothing in Heidegger, Daoism, and Buddhism.

If we distinguish the conceptions of nothing into these three basic types, then Heidegger's and Daoism's conception of nothing can be characterized as "original nothing." The unique Daoist cosmogonical-ontological approach renders nothing more "original" than its parallels in Western philosophy. In contrast, the emptiness in Madhyamaka Buddhism is basically a type of privative nothing, but its tendency to negate all existents at the ultimate level leads to negative nothing. And finally, the emptiness in Yogācāra Buddhism is basically nothing as absence or privation, but its affirmation of ultimate reality leads to original nothing. The latter sense of emptiness was more influential among East Asian Buddhists, and more easily confused with the Daoists' original nothing. With this analysis, I hope to clarify some confusion in the understanding of nothing in Heidegger, Daoism, and Buddhism.

This typology of nothing also sheds light on the central philosophical issue of "what there is not." The perplexity of this issue is attributed to the fact that nonbeing or nothing, by its very nature, escapes from falling into a being or something and thus resists any attempt at definition or characterization. In the history of philosophy, the mystery of nothing is usually associated with an equally mysterious question. That is, why, according to Parmenides and the Sarvāstivādins, can we not think or talk about nonbeing? This question becomes even more intriguing in contrast to the fact that we can talk about nonbeing or nothing with ease in our ordinary language.

According to my typology of nothing, when Parmenides and the Sarvāstivādins forbade us from thinking or talking about nonbeing, they were warning us against the altogether not or absolute nothing, for example, square-circle and the son of a barren woman. It is evident that this type of nothing was mainly a logician's concern, including Moists, Hindu and Buddhist logicians, and contemporary analytic philosophers. Given its nature of being logically contradictory and impossible, this type of nothing, as predicted by Parmenides, does not really enter into the realm of knowledge, but rather functions as an indicator of the limit of human knowledge. What does enter into the realm of our knowledge and ordinary language is a different type of nothing. To break the curse of Parmenides, Plato and his followers were approaching "what there is not" in the sense of "difference" or "*x* is absent of *y*." In the Indian context, the Mahāsāṃghika, Yogācāras, and Sautrāntikas were mainly concerned with the past and the future, which can also be understood as absence. This absence or privation of being, as another type of nothing, is always an essential part of our knowledge. So the reason that we can think or talk about nonbeing or nothing with ease is not because Parmenides and the Sarvāstivādins were wrong, but because we are approaching a different interpretation of nothing.

PART ONE

COGNITION OF NONEXISTENT OBJECTS: A HISTORICAL DEVELOPMENT

1

Mahāsāṃghika

The present chapter will explore some pre-Vaibhāṣika sources that are extant in Pāli and Chinese, including the *Kathāvatthu*, *Samayabhedoparacanacakra*, *Śāriputrābhidharma*, and *Vijñānakāya*. These scattered sources suggest an early origin of the concept of the cognition of nonexistent objects among the Mahāsāṃghikas and some Vibhajyavādins under their influence. They also indicate some different aspects of this theory from that held by the Dārṣṭāntika-Sautrāntikas. In particular, some Mahāsāṃghika arguments reveal how a soteriologically oriented concept of cognition without objects gradually develops into the sophisticated philosophical concept of the cognition of nonexistent objects. This again, to echo my conclusion on the study of self-cognition (*svasaṃvedana*) (Yao 2005), shows that the concept of the cognition of nonexistent objects has an origin in the soteriological discourse, and that many Mahāsāṃghika theories have great impact on the later development of Buddhist doctrinal systems.

1.1 Latent Defilements without Objects

The first Mahāsāṃghika argument for the cognition of nonexistent objects has to do with *anuśaya*, a generic term for defilements. But in its usage, it is more appropriate to translate it into "latent defilements." It is well documented that the Mahāsāṃghikas disagreed with the Sarvāstivādins (and possibly other Sthaviravāda schools) on the relationship between *anuśaya* and *paryavasthāna* (the manifested defilements). In his *Samayabhedoparacanacakra*, Vasumitra lists the following statement as one of the main doctrines shared by the Mahāsāṃghikas and its sub-schools, including Ekavyavahārika, Lokottaravāda, and Kaukkuṭika: "*Anuśaya* is not a mind or mental activity, and it has no objects. *Anuśaya* is distinguished from *paryavasthāna*, and *paryavasthāna* is distinguished from *anuśaya*. It should be said that *anuśaya* is not associated with the mind, while *paryavasthāna* is associated with the mind."[1]

The same statement is found among the shared doctrines of the Mahīśāsakas and its sub-school Dharmaguptaka.[2] These schools are the major components of the so-called Vibhajyavādins.[3] It is possible that the Vibhajyavādins were influenced by the Mahāsāṃghikas on this point, and this agreement between the two parties is the basis for their contributions to the development of the theory of cognition of nonexistent objects.

In contrast to the Mahāsāṃghika and Vibhajyavāda view on *anuśaya* and *paryavasthāna*, the Sarvāstivādins held the exactly opposite view: "All *anuśaya*s are mental activities, associated with the mind, and have objects. All *anuśaya*s are included in *paryavasthāna*, but not all *paryavasthāna*s are included in *anuśaya*."[4] Similar views are found in a more elaborate form in Sarvāstivāda Abhidharma works such as *Mahāvibhāṣā*, *Nyāyānusāra*, and *Abhidharmakośabhāṣya*.[5]

This debate involves some issues with great soteriological implications. Liberation, the goal of Buddhist practice, is meant to be free from defilements (*anuśaya*). Therefore, *anuśaya* undoubtedly occupies a central position in the Buddhist soteriology, and the understanding and analysis of defilements constitute the essential part of the Buddhist doctrinal system. Schools such as Mahāsāṃghika and Mahīśāsaka held that a finer analysis should be made to distinguish between *anuśaya* and *paryavasthāna*, the latent and manifested defilements. This distinction is applicable to many soteriological issues, including the possibility of retrogression, an issue hotly debated among sectarian Buddhists.[6] As I am not mainly concerned with soteriological issues in the current study, I am not going to further discuss how this distinction between latent and manifested defilements is applied to solve or evoke various soteriological problems. Instead, I am interested in how this distinction is made. It is suggested that the Mahāsāṃghikas and Mahīśāsakas made this distinction on the following ground: *Anuśaya* is not associated with the mind, while *paryavasthāna* is. In other words, *anuśaya* or the latent defilement that is disjoined from the mind is not a mental activity. In contrast, *paryavasthāna* or the manifested defilement that is conjoined with the mind is a mental activity. So the line is clear: *anuśaya* is not a mental activity, but *paryavasthāna* is.

In his commentary on the *Samayabhedoparacanacakra*, Kuiji (窺基) explains the reason for the Mahāsāṃghika view that *anuśaya* is not a mental activity. First of all, *anuśaya* consists of ten types of defilements: desire (*rāga*), enmity (*pratigha*), ignorance (*avidyā*), conceit (*māna*), doubt (*vicikitsā*), self-view (*satkāyadṛṣṭi*), extreme view (*antagrāhadṛṣṭi*), false view (*mithyādṛṣṭi*), adherence to one's own views (*dṛṣṭi-parāmarśa*), and adherence to abstentions and vows (*śīla-vrata-parāmarśa*).[7] It accompanies the ordinary person (*pṛthagjana*) all the time, even in her state of mindless meditation (*asaṃjñi-samāpatti*) or in her mental state that is morally good.[8] The state of mindless meditation is especially important for the Mahāsāṃghikas to develop their view on *anuśaya*. It is believed to be a state in which all the mind and mental activities cease to function. The fact that the mind and mental activities can resume after the state of mindless meditation contributed greatly to the development of the concept of store consciousness (*ālaya-vijñāna*) later among the Yogācāras. The Mahāsāṃghikas, however, are more concerned with what happens in the state of mindless meditation. As it is a state accessible to an ordinary person through proper training, there must be defilements in it. Otherwise, those who are in the state of mindless meditation would be the liberated persons (*arhat*) rather than ordinary ones. As we know, according to the Buddhist soteriology, the key difference between the liberated persons and the ordinary person is whether they are accompanied by defilements. So the Mahāsāṃghikas admit that the defilements that pertain through mindless meditation must not be mental activities. As a result, we have to distinguish between *paryavasthāna*, the manifested defilements that are associated with the mind, and *anuśaya*, the latent defilements that are not mental activities.

Believing in a nonmental latent defilement is a view shared by the Mahāsāṃghikas and its sub-schools (including Ekavyavahārika, Lokottaravāda, and Kaukkuṭika), the Mahīśāsakas and its sub-school Dharmaguptaka, and the Saṃmatīyas.[9] For some, especially the Sarvāstivādins, this view is unacceptable. How can desire and so on, which are usually considered to be typical mental activities, be nonmental? They hold firmly that "all the latent defilements (*anuśaya*) are mental activities and associated with the mind."[10] Meanwhile, they do not make a sharp distinction between *anuśaya* and *paryavasthāna*, and consider both to be the epithets of *kleśa* (defilements).

Anuśaya, either mental or nonmental, is understood to be a human disposition with the characteristic of increasing or decreasing along with its objects. For instance, one's desire may increase when encountering a favorable object and decrease when meeting with an unfavorable one. Understanding the interaction between defilements and their objects is a very important aspect of Buddhist practice that aims to eliminate these defilements. And the practice consists of internally calming down the defilements and externally avoiding objects that help the growth of defilements. Now the Mahāsāṃghikas have to face a serious challenge: If *anuśaya* is nonmental, how can it have an object? If it has no objects, how can it maintain its growth? Again, it is well documented that the Mahāsāṃghikas and its sub-schools, including Ekavyavahārika, Lokottaravāda, and Kaukkuṭika, exclaimed that "[*anuśaya*] has no objects either."[11] The Mahīśāsakas and its sub-school Dharmaguptaka adopted the same view, and the Sarvāstivādins, accordingly, went against such a view by insisting that "[*anuśaya*] has objects."[12]

It is evident that the Theravādins also argued against this view. As a matter of fact, their debate with the Andhakas and some Uttarāpathakas on the subject, as found in *Kathāvatthu* IX.4, constitutes the most substantial material for the current discussion.[13] First of all, this text indicates that seven types of *anuśaya* (Pāli: *anusaya*) are under discussion: sensual desire (*kāmarāga*), enmity (*paṭigha*), conceit (*māna*), erroneous opinion (*diṭṭha*), doubt (*vicikicchā*), desire of life (*bhavarāga*), and ignorance (*avijjā*). On the view of the Andhakas, the *anuśaya* of desire (latent desire) is distinguished from manifested desire, the desire as outburst (*kāmarāgapariyuṭṭhāna*), bond (*kāmarāgasaññojana*), flood (*kāmogha*), fetter (*kāmayoga*), or obstacle (*kāmacchandanīvaraṇa*), all of which are the manifestations of desire in different degrees. The latent desire has no objects, while the rest have. The reason for this is not that *anuśaya* belongs to material form, sense organs, or sense objects, all of which are part of the material realm and certainly possess no objects. Nor is it because *anuśaya* belongs to *nirvāṇa*, the unconditioned state that goes beyond material and mental factors, and the division between subject and object. Instead, *anuśaya* is associated with conditioning force (*saṅkhāra*, *saṃskāra*).

The text then discusses more extensively how *anuśaya* is associated with conditioning force. On the one hand, if the latent desire belongs to *saṅkhāra*, then *saṅkhāra* should also be without objects. On the other hand, however, the manifested desire itself also belongs to *saṅkhāra*, and this desire certainly possesses objects, and therefore *saṅkhāra* should have objects. The Andhakas are forced into a self-contradiction by admitting *saṅkhāra* to be both with and without objects. Their solution to this contradiction is to admit "a portion of *saṅkhāra* being with objects and the other portion without objects."[14] Buddhaghosa explains that the *saṅkhāra* with objects refers to the aggregate of *saṅkhāra* that is associated with the mind (*citta-sampayutta-saṅkhāra-kkhandha*), while the *saṅkhāra* without objects is meant to cover other factors included in *saṅkhāra*, such as latent defilements (*anusaya*), vitality (*jīvitindriya*), and forms of bodily actions (*kāyakammādirūpa*).[15] As we know, the latter group of concepts developed into a separate category of the conditionings disassociated with the mind (*citta-viprayukta-saṃskāra*) among the Sarvāstivādins. Although they disagree among themselves on the number of concepts included in this category, they unanimously exclude *anuśaya* from the list because they believe, as we discussed earlier, *anuśaya* is associated with the mind and has objects.

When the Andhakas were asked whether this division between the portion associated with the mind and that disassociated from it is applicable to other aggregates such as feeling (*vedanā*), conception (*saññā*), and consciousness (*viññāṇa*), they replied in the negative. This means that only the aggregate of *saṅkhāra* enjoys the status of being both associated and disassociated with the mind. Interestingly enough, a parallel view is found in the *Śāriputrābhidharma*, an early Abhidharma work believed to be associated with the Mahīśāsakas and the Dharmaguptakas.[16] The text states:

> What is the one which is of two portions—either associated with or disassociated with the mind? It is the aggregate of conditioning force (*saṃskāra*) . . . What is [the portion of] the aggregate of conditioning force which is disassociated with the mind? It is [the portion of] the aggregate of conditioning force which is not mental activities, i.e., life (*jāti*), etc., up to the attainment of cessation (*nirodha-samāpatti*).[17]

Since the list is shortened, we do not know whether it includes *anuśaya* or not, but Cox (1995: 76 n19) suggests that it may do.

Finally, the Andhakas argue for the latent defilements being without objects along the line of moral psychology. When the ordinary person, that is, one who has not been liberated from defilements, is willing something morally good (*kusala*) or neutral (*abyākata*), she is still understood to be embedded with *anuśaya*, for otherwise she will be liberated.[18] In this state, her good or neutral thoughts have their corresponding objects, but her latent defilements at that moment cannot have any objects. If they do, the morally bad thought would emerge and that would eradicate any morally good or neutral thought.

This argument in terms of moral psychology makes more sense if we understand *anuśaya* as an unconscious or subconscious state. An unconscious or subconscious state can be understood to be disassociated with the conscious mind, so it is not a regular type of mental activity. Therefore, it does not take the normal mental objects as its objects and can be considered to have no objects. Another way to make sense of this point is to resort to the Lacanian concept of pure desire that is beyond any recognizable object. For Lacan, desire is not a relation to an object but a relation to a lack (*manque*). In any case, the thesis that latent defilements have no objects constitutes the first step toward the formation of the concept of the cognition of nonexistent objects.

1.2 Awareness without Objects

The second argument for the cognition of nonexistent objects that is associated with the Mahāsāṃghikas and its sub-schools has to do with awareness (*ñāṇa*). So far, the most extensive source for such an argument is found in the *Kathāvatthu* IX.5, where a debate between the Theravādins and the Andhakas is reported. This section has a similar structure as the section we discussed earlier. First, the Andhakas distinguish awareness from wisdom (*paññā*), wisdom faculty (*paññindriya*), wisdom power (*paññābala*), right view (*sammādiṭṭhi*), and discernment as a limb of enlightenment (*dhamma-vicaya-saṃbojjh-aṅga*), all of which are believed to have objects. Awareness, however, is assumed to have no objects. The reason for this is not that awareness is associated with material form, sense organs, or sense objects, all of which have no objects. Nor is it because awareness is associated with *nirvāṇa*, which is beyond material and mental factors and certainly has no objects. Awareness is rather associated with the aggregate of *saṅkhāra*.

If awareness is assumed to have no objects and to be associated with the aggregate of *saṅkhāra*, then the *saṅkhāra* itself as a whole should have no objects. But the Andhakas admit that the wisdom that possesses objects is also associated with the aggregate of *saṅkhāra*, and therefore *saṅkhāra* is considered to have objects. To resolve the contradiction that *saṅkhāra* is both with and without objects, the Andhakas admit that one portion of *saṅkhāra* has objects, while the other portion does not. This division, again, is applicable only to the aggregate of *saṅkhāra*, but not to other aggregates such as feeling, conception, and consciousness, all of which are believed to have objects all the time.

In the *Kathāvatthu* XI.3, a similar pattern of argument is employed to argue that awareness is not associated with the mind (*citta*). Buddhaghosa attributed this view to the Pubbaseliyas, a sub-school of the Andhakas. These two sets of arguments with regard to awareness, though attributed to different branches of the Mahāsāṃghikas, are related to each other. If awareness is associated with the mind, then it certainly should have objects. If, however, awareness is not associated with the mind, then it is understandably without objects. But a difficult point is how to understand the awareness disassociated with the mind, for this concept contradicts our usual understanding of awareness (*ñāṇa*), which can be anything other than a mental activity. In the various lists of conditionings disassociated with the mind (*citta-viprayukta-saṃskāra*) developed among the later Sarvāstivādins, awareness has not been included.

To fully understand this point, we have to look at the rest of the argument, which involves the relationship between awareness and consciousness (*viññāṇa*). Being a pair of concepts that are widely circulated in Buddhist doctrinal system, awareness and consciousness have a complicated relationship. In the Sarvāstivāda Abhidharma system, extensive sources indicate that they are used in many cases interchangeably. When distinguished, they are believed to be associated with different realms: awareness being undefiled and a mental activity (*caitta*), while consciousness is defiled and synonymous with the mind (*citta*).[19] In the earlier debates among various Buddhist schools as recorded in the *Kathāvatthu*, we see some other aspects of the relationship between awareness and consciousness. In the *Kathāvatthu* IX.5 and XI.3, both the Andhakas and the Pubbaseliyas argue that an *arhat*, after the attainment of the knowledge of path (*magga*), is believed to "possess awareness" (*ñāṇīti*) at all time from then on. This is also the case when she is engaged in a sense consciousness. For instance, when she perceives something, fully engaged in the visual experience, her awareness is also active.[20] In this process, the visual consciousness has visual objects as its objects, but the awareness, the Andhakas and the Pubbaseliyas conclude, should have no objects. The reason for this is probably that there cannot be two objects of cognition at the same instant of time.

As the account in the *Kathāvatthu* is too brief, we do not know for sure the context of this argument. One possibility is to understand it in the context of the Andhaka arguments for reflexive awareness. As I discussed elsewhere (Yao 2005: 15–33), the Andhakas and some other schools of the Mahāsāṃghika origin hold that the mind is aware of itself while acting on external objects. In this process, the sense consciousness that acts on sensory objects is working at the same time when a certain awareness is active. I call it a reflexive model of self-awareness in contrast to the reflective model of self-awareness propounded among the Sarvāstivādins. The latter model is thus named because the Sarvāstivādins hold that self-awareness is possible only in the later moment when the mind reflects the sensory experience. In the Mahāsāṃghika model, however, the awareness is active at the same time as the sensory experience. While the sensory consciousness takes sensory objects as its objects, the awareness ends up with no objects, because it is believed that no two objects can be presented at the same time, although for the Mahāsāṃghikas two mental processes can take place at the same time.

This discussion with reference to self-awareness may only indicate one way of making sense of the Andhaka argument that awareness has no objects. To seek alternative ways of understanding, we have to take into account the

Pubbaseliya view that awareness is disassociated with the mind. This view, to a great extent, contradicts our usual understanding of awareness, but it is not entirely unimaginable. In the later Buddhist epistemological tradition, the concepts of mere non-perception (*adarśanamātra*) and non-cognition (*anupalabdhi*) were developed to account for the cognition of negative facts. One of the salient features of this means of knowledge is indicated by the inactiveness of other means of knowledge such as perception and inference (see Chapter 5). If following this line of thought, the awareness disassociated with the mind can be understood as a state in which all mental activities are ceased. This nonmental awareness is not entirely a blackout, rather it could be, similar to the case of non-perception or non-cognition, responsible for the cognition of negative facts. When it is said that awareness is without objects, it really means that it does not take the normal existent objects as its objects, but rather it has *nonexistent* objects as its objects.

The connection between the awareness without objects and the awareness of nonexistent objects seems to be supported by a pre-Vaibhāṣika source from the *Śāriputrābhidharma*. This work is believed to be the earliest Abhidharma work in the Northern tradition of Indian Buddhism, but its received version in Chinese reflects more of the Mahīśāsaka and Dharmaguptaka views. While enumerating various types of awareness (*jñāna*), this text lists "the awareness of nonexistent objects" (*wu jingjie zhi* 無境界智, **asadālambanajñāna*) as one of more than two hundred types of awareness.[21] The first thing to be noted is that it is called an "awareness" (*jñāna*) of nonexistent objects, which echoes the Andhaka arguments with respect to awareness, though we are not sure whether the "awareness" here is associated with the mind. Later in the text, two definitions of this concept are given. The first definition reads: "What is the awareness of nonexistent objects? That which has no objects (**anālambana*) is the awareness of nonexistent objects."[22] Contemporary scholars, including Sakamoto (1981: 135) and Cox (1988: 44), took the first definition as a denial of this concept: "There is *no* awareness of nonexistent objects."[23] But this denial contradicts the fact that it is listed earlier in the text as one type of awareness. My interpretation, in contrast, makes it clear that the awareness of nonexistent objects is defined as "the awareness that has *no objects*."

1.3 Consciousness of the Past and the Future

The third argument for the cognition of nonexistent objects is related to the consciousness of the past and the future. Unlike the first two arguments that were to a great extent neglected by later Buddhists, this argument became one of the focal points in the Sautrāntika-Sarvāstivāda debates. It is interesting to note that the Dārṣṭāntikas did not explore the argument with this respect when they argued for the cognition of nonexistent objects (see Chapter 2). It can be explained by the fact that the Dārṣṭāntikas still, following the line of the Sarvāstivādins, believe in the existence of past and future factors. This also helps us to draw a line between the Dārṣṭāntikas and the Sautrāntikas, at least on this point.

Buddhaghosa attributed the argument for the consciousness of the past and the future to the Uttarāpathakas.[24] In this argument, a key term to be noted is "consciousness" (*citta*). As compared to the latent defilements (*anuśaya*) and the awareness (*ñāṇa*) that we discussed earlier, consciousness is unambiguously mental and conscious. So the consciousness recalling a past object (*atītārammaṇaṃ cittaṃ*) is a cognition of the object on a conscious level.[25] The central thesis that the Uttarāpathakas argue for can be stated as follows: "The consciousness that [recalls] a past object or [anticipates] a future object is [a consciousness] without objects."[26] In the eyes of their opponents, that is, the Theravādins, however, this is a self-contradictory statement. As they have already talked about the consciousness being involved with a past object (*atītārammaṇa*) or a future object (*anāgatārammaṇa*), how can they say that the consciousness is "without objects" (*anārammaṇa*)? Moreover, there is still adverting of consciousness (*āvaṭṭanā*), ideation, coordinated application, attention, volition, anticipation, or aiming at (*paṇidhi*) concerning that which is past or future; therefore, how is it possible that the consciousness in these states is without objects? If the Uttarāpathakas want to be consistent, the Theravādins urge, they should also admit that the consciousness perceiving a present object is the consciousness without objects. But they would not go so far to deny the existence of the present object. Instead, they insist that the basic reason for the consciousness that involves with a past or future object being the consciousness without objects is that "the past and the future do not exist."[27] Therefore, when the consciousness is attending or aiming at a present object, it is a consciousness with objects; when the consciousness is attending or aiming at a past or future object, it is a consciousness without objects.

As the Theravādins agreed with the Uttarāpathakas and many other Buddhist schools in propounding the view that past and future factors do not exist, they did not get into further debate on this point. But the Theravādins' accusation of their opponents being self-contradictory still makes sense. If past and future factors do not exist, it is impossible to talk about "a past object" (*atītārammaṇa*) or "a future object" (*anāgatārammaṇa*) in the first place, and it evokes a self-contradiction to say that "the consciousness recalling a past object is a consciousness without objects." This desperate situation is similar to what contemporary philosophers called the Meinongian paradox—a paradox involving virtually all types of negative existential statements. This instance shows that Buddhist philosophers were aware of the difficulty involved with such an issue.

Besides the *Kathāvatthu*, we have a few more pre-Vaibhāṣika sources that argue for the cognition of nonexistent objects along the line of the consciousness of the past and the future. In the *Śāriputrābhidharma*, the second definition of the awareness of nonexistent objects reads: "What is the awareness of nonexistent objects? . . . Or, the arising of the awareness that contends to past or future factors is called the awareness of nonexistent objects."[28] This definition is evidently related to the Uttarāpathaka argument regarding the consciousness of the past and the future. As we know the received version of *Śāriputrābhidharma* is associated with the Mahīśāsakas and the Dharmaguptakas, then, most probably, this concept originated in the Mahāsāṃghika subgroup Uttarāpathaka and was accepted and further developed among the Vibhajyavādins, including the Mahīśāsakas and the Dharmaguptakas.

Later in the *Śāriputrābhidharma*, while enumerating various types of meditation, a meditation of nonexistent objects (*wu jingjie ding* 無境界定, **asadālambanasamādhi*) is listed as one of more than two hundred types of meditation.[29] Later in the text, two definitions of this concept are given: (1) the meditation that has no objects; (2) the meditation that contemplates on past or future factors.[30] We have not encountered this concept in our earlier discussions. It may indicate another possible origin for the Buddhist theory of the cognition of nonexistent objects. Besides the soteriological and epistemological approaches that we have discussed earlier, the meditative practice undoubtedly occupies a central position in the Buddhist tradition, and it is understandable that Buddhist practitioners would develop their theory of the cognition of nonexistent objects on the basis of their relevant meditative experience.

The other early source is the *Vijñānakāya*, one of the "six limbs" of Sarvāstivāda Abhidharma works. Being attributed to Devaśarman, this work begins with the refutation of the views of a certain Maudgalyāyana. It is repeatedly stated that Maudgalyāyana holds that things of the past and the future do not exist, but the present and the unconditioned do.[31] In his *Samayabhedoparacanacakra*, Vasumitra reports that this view was shared by the Mahīśāsakas and its subgroup Dharmaguptaka.[32] According to the same text, the Dharmaguptakas claim themselves to be the followers of Maudgalyāyana.[33] So we can assume that the Maudgalyāyana mentioned in the *Vijñānakāya* is this Dharmaguptaka Maudgalyāyana.

Among the various views of Maudgalyāyana refuted by Devaśarman, one is reported as follows: "There is the consciousness (*xin* 心, **citta*) of nonexistent objects."[34] It is worth noting that the key term "consciousness" is used, which indicates that the faculty for the cognition of nonexistent objects is the consciousness itself. It is also coherent to the Uttarāpathaka usage of "the *consciousness* without objects" (*cittaṃ anārammaṇan*), which was discussed earlier in this section. More importantly, Maudgalyāyana further explains the reason for admitting this consciousness of nonexistent objects as follows: "There must be the consciousness of nonexistent objects. Why? Because the consciousness cognizes the past or the future."[35] This view is in turn built upon their shared assumption that "the past and the future do not exist," which is refuted extensively by Devaśarman in the *Vijñānakāya*.

In any case, the Sarvāstivādins supplied us some scattered sources that reveal the connection between the Uttarāpathakas and the Dharmaguptakas on the understanding of the cognition of nonexistent objects as the cognition of the past and the future. This view was probably also shared by some other Mahāsāṃghika and Vibhajyavāda subgroups. Without further evidence, we cannot explore further. But it is evident that the later Sautrāntikas (but not the Dārṣṭāntikas) further developed this view by heavily engaging debates with the Vaibhāṣikas on the cognition of the past and the future (see Chapter 4).

1.4 Three Arguments

Based on scattered sources in Pāli and Chinese, we have reconstructed three arguments for the cognition of nonexistent objects that are associated with the Mahāsāṃghikas and some Vibhajyavādins under their influence. In the first argument, the thesis reads: "Latent defilements (*anuśaya*) have no objects."[36] The Mahāsāṃghikas and its sub-schools (including Ekavyavahārika, Lokottaravāda, and Kaukkuṭika), the Mahīśāsakas and its sub-school Dharmaguptaka, and the Saṃmatīyas were arguing for this view, while the Sarvāstivādins (and possibly other Sthaviravāda schools) were arguing against it. The proponents formulate four main reasons to support their thesis: (1) latent defilements (*anuśaya*) are distinguished from manifested defilements (*paryavasthāna*); (2) latent defilements are not associated with the mind (*citta*), nor are they a mental activity (*caitta*), but rather they are associated with conditioning force (*saṃskāra*), and possibly components of conditionings disassociated with the mind (*citta-viprayukta-saṃskāra*); (3) latent defilements accompany an ordinary person (*pṛthagjana*) at all times, even in her state of mindless meditation; (4) when an ordinary person is willing something morally good or neutral, her good or neutral thoughts have their corresponding objects, but the latent defilements at that moment cannot have any object. To make sense of this argument from a contemporary perspective, we have resorted to the Freudian concept of unconscious or subconscious and the Lacanian concept of pure desire without objects.

In the second argument, the thesis is expressed in two different ways: (1) "Awareness (*ñāṇa*) has no objects"[37]; or (2) "The awareness that has no objects (**anālambana*) is the awareness of nonexistent objects."[38] The Andhakas, Pubbaseliyas, and Dharmaguptakas were the proponents, while the Theravādins were their opponents. The proponents provide three reasons to support their thesis: (1) awareness is distinguished from wisdom (*paññā*); (2) awareness is not associated with the mind (*citta*), nor is it a mental activity (*caitta*), but rather it is associated with conditioning force (*saṃskāra*), and might also be a component of conditionings disassociated with the mind (*citta-viprayukta-saṃskāra*); (3) when an *arhat* perceives something, fully engaged in the visual experience, her awareness is also active. In this process, the visual consciousness has visual objects as its objects, but the awareness should have no objects. To make sense of this argument, we have discussed the Mahāsāṃghika theory of reflexive awareness, according to which awareness is active while the subject engages visual or other sensory experience. Moreover, their concept of "awareness disassociated with the mind" anticipates the concept of non-cognition in Buddhist epistemology, which is a state of mind that other means of knowledge such as perception and inference are inactive.

In the third argument, the thesis is expressed in various different ways: (1) "The consciousness (*citta*) that [recalls] a past object or [anticipates] a future object is [the consciousness] without objects"[39]; or (2) "The arising of the awareness (*jñāna*) that contends to past or future factors is called the awareness of nonexistent objects"[40]; or (3) "There must be the consciousness (*citta*) of nonexistent objects. Why? Because the consciousness cognizes past or future [factors]."[41] The reason given by the proponents, that is, the Uttarāpathakas and the Dharmaguptakas, is simple, that is, "because the past and the future do not exist." Although agreeing with this reason, their opponents—the Theravādins—point out a paradox involving virtually all negative existential statements: If past and future factors do not exist, it is impossible to talk about "a past object" (*atītārammaṇa*) or "a future object" (*anāgatārammaṇa*) in the first place. So it is self-contradictory to say: "The consciousness recalling a past object is the consciousness without objects."

As compared to the other arguments for the cognition of nonexistent objects developed later by the Dārṣṭāntika-Sautrāntikas and the Yogācāras, these three arguments of Mahāsāṃghika origin are more primitive. But they reveal some features of this theory in its early development. In particular, the x of nonexistent objects is evolved from x without objects. In the case of latent defilements, it is the latent defilements without objects. But when it comes to awareness, it can be the awareness without objects or the awareness of nonexistent objects. The consciousness of the past and the future is more explicitly the cognition of nonexistent objects in the past and the future.

2

Dārṣṭāntika

In the voluminous *Mahāvibhāṣā* (MV), I found some scattered sources on the cognition of nonexistent objects, which are exclusively attributed to the Dārṣṭāntikas, a subgroup of Sarvāstivāda. The Vaibhāṣikas, whose were the composers of MV, had knowledge of many Mahāsāṃghika doctrines and, in many cases, fiercely argued against them. But it seems that they did not take the concept of the cognition of nonexistent objects as a major doctrine of Mahāsāṃghika. Instead, they refuted it as one of the main doctrines of the Dārṣṭāntikas. The possible scenario could be that around the time when MV was composed the Dārṣṭāntikas accepted this Mahāsāṃghika concept and developed it into one of their main doctrines. As I will show in this chapter, in the hands of the Dārṣṭāntikas, as recorded in Harivarman's **Janakaparamopadeśa* (JP)[1] and refuted in MV and in Saṃghabhadra's *Nyāyānusāra* (NA), this concept has entered a new stage of development.

2.1 Objects of Conjunction and Feeling

A characteristic feature of the Mahāsāṃghika concept of the cognition of nonexistent objects is that it begins with an emotional aspect of human mind, *anuśaya* or latent defilements. We do not have evidence for whether the Dārṣṭāntikas accepted the Mahāsāṃghika distinction between latent defilements (*anuśaya*) and manifested defilements (*paryavasthāna*). But in MV, the Dārṣṭāntikas do discuss the ontological status of objects of the defilement, which they call conjunction (*saṃyoga*).

To argue against the Sarvāstivāda view that both conjunction and its objects are real existence, the Dārṣṭāntikas hold that conjunction is real, but its objects are unreal. It is reported in MV: "They [=Dārṣṭāntikas] hold that the objects may or may not generate defilements as they do not have a fixed nature. Therefore, these objects are known to be unreal (*feishi* 非實)."[2] This view is illustrated with the example of a beautiful woman. On seeing her, some feel respect, some greed, some hatred, some jealousy, some disgust, some compassion, and some equanimity. In this example, the Dārṣṭāntikas seem not to deny the actual existence of the woman herself. Being an object of perception ("on seeing *her*"), she actually exists. But she cannot function simultaneously as the object of conflicting emotional states such as respect, greed, hatred, and so on. Based on this observation, the Dārṣṭāntikas infer that the objects of mental defilements do not really exist, and conclude that "accordingly one knows the objects (*jing* 境, **viṣaya*) [of conjunction] do not exist as real entities."[3]

Reflecting this Dārṣṭāntika argument from a contemporary perspective, one would find that the Dārṣṭāntikas have confused between the content and the object of a cognition, or between intentional objects and external objects. The thesis they try to prove is that "the content (*vastu*) of [conjunction] is unreal."[4] The supportive example of a beauty works fine, but the Dārṣṭāntikas jump too quickly and illegitimately to the conclusion that "objects (**viṣaya*) do not exist as real entities." As we have discussed earlier, the "object" here cannot be the object of perception, that is, the beauty herself. If it were so, the Dārṣṭāntikas would commit to idealism that even denies the existence of the object of *perception*. Therefore, their conclusion should only mean to say that "the objects of *conjunction* do not exist as real entities." In other words, the content or intentional object of conjunction (*saṃyoga-vastu*) is not an independent object.

Vastu, literally meaning "things" or "entities," can cover a broader scope of "content" or "intentional objects," whereas *viṣaya* primarily refers to external independent objects. The subtle distinction between the two concepts can also be found in a theory of feeling (*vedanā*) attributed to the Bhadanta Dharmatrāta, one of the leading Dārṣṭāntikas during the period when MV was composed. He distinguishes two types of feeling: bodily and mental. According to him, whatever is a bodily feeling is also a mental feeling, but not vice versa. This means that some mental feelings are not bodily feeling. The Dārṣṭāntikas further clarify that "all those [mental] feelings, without grasping external things (*shi* 事, **vastu*), give rise to conceptual constructions (*vikalpa*); depending solely on internal things (*shi* 事, **vastu*), they grasp their forms and give rise to conceptual constructions."[5]

This distinction between external and internal things (**vastu*) is helpful for us to understand Dharmatrāta's theory of feeling. The external things are objects of bodily feeling that really exist, whereas the internal things are the conceptually constructed objects of mental feeling. The association of feeling (*vedanā*) with conceptual construction (*vikalpa*) needs further explanation because feeling is usually taken to be sensory, and hence devoid of conceptual construction. This is true for bodily feeling. But Dharmatrāta's sense of mental feeling, with its capacity of conceptual construction, is similar to mental consciousness. This is evident in a few examples of mental feeling that he mentions later in the text: "The mental feeling is thus named because it takes as objects (*ālambante*) that all persons (*pudgala*) are existent, and also takes as objects the matter (*rūpa*) subsumed under the sphere of *dharma* (*dharmāyatana*), [i.e., the unmanifested matter (*avijñapti-rūpa*)], the conditionings disassociated with mind (*citta-viprayukta-saṃskāra*), the unconditioned *dharmas*, etc."[6]

All these objects seem to be proper objects of mental consciousness rather than those of sensation or feeling. The Vaibhāṣikas also comment that "the Bhadanta intends that such mental feeling has no real objects and is merely the operation of conceptual construction."[7] In light of these comments, we realize that Dharmatrāta's sense of "internal things" is not "real objects." If "external things" refer to real existent objects, then "internal things" are those unreal and nonexistent objects that are the proper objects of conceptual construction and of mental feeling.

Reexamining the aforementioned examples of the objects of mental feeling, we shall realize that, according to Dharmatrāta, all those objects of mental feeling—for instance, persons, the unmanifested matter, the conditionings disassociated with mind, and the unconditioned *dharma*s—are unreal and nonexistent. The Vaibhāṣikas, however, may agree with Dharmatrāta that persons do not exist, but they would not admit that the other three types of objects are nonexistent. Dharmatrāta has deviated from the orthodox Vaibhāṣika position by denying the existence of the unmanifested matter, the conditionings disassociated with mind, and the unconditioned *dharma*s, which is a view inhered by the Dārṣṭāntikas and Sautrāntikas. Meanwhile, he has established the concept of the mental feeling of nonexistent objects through denying the existence of these objects.

2.2 Illusions

In MV, the most explicit expression of the cognition of nonexistent objects is found in the following passage: "Some, such as the Dārṣṭāntikas, hold that there is the awareness of nonexistent objects (*yuan wu zhi* 緣無智, **asadālambanajñāna*). They say that the awareness (*jñāna*) that takes as objects illusions, the imaginary city Gandharva, fire-wheel, mirage, and etc., is the awareness of nonexistent objects."[8] Here, the first thing to be noted is that the Dārṣṭāntikas use the term "*awareness* (*jñāna*) of nonexistent objects." As we saw in the previous chapter, this term was used by the Mahīśāsakas and Dharmaguptakas in the *Śāriputrābhidharma* and could also be found among the Mahāsāṃghikas and its sub-schools when they argued for the thesis that "awareness (*ñāṇa*) has no objects" in the *Kathāvatthu* IX.5. In later sources for the Dārṣṭāntika-Sautrāntika arguments for this concept, their emphasis is shifted to the *consciousness* (*vijñāna*) of nonexistent objects in the *Abhidharmakośabhāṣya* (AKBh) and **Nyāyānusāra* (NA).

Elsewhere in MV, it discusses the concept of "cognition without objects":

> Some hold that there are various kinds of cognition (*juehui* 覺慧, **buddhi*) that have no objects (*wu suoyuan jing* 無所緣境). For instance, the various kinds of cognition apprehend illusions, the imaginary city of Gandharva, mirror-images, moon reflected on the surface of water, shadow, mirage, fire-wheel, and etc. All of them have no real objects (*wu shi jing* 無實境).[9]

Although this statement is not explicitly attributed to the Dārṣṭāntikas, judging from the parallel examples in the list, we can safely assume that the Dārṣṭāntikas would endorse the concept of "the cognition without objects" and use it in the sense of "the cognition of nonexistent objects."

Why can awareness (*jñāna*) or cognition (*buddhi*) apprehend nonexistent objects? Unlike the Mahāsāṃghikas who explore the possible states of the awareness disassociated with mind and of reflexive awareness in their arguments for awareness without objects, the Dārṣṭāntikas resort to a great variety of optical illusions. Their arguments for the cognition of nonexistent objects rely heavily on the ontological status of these illusory objects. If they are nonexistent, then the Dārṣṭāntika concept of the cognition of nonexistent objects is proved. If, however, these are actually existent objects, then their opponents, Vaibhāṣikas, win the debate. In MV, it reports the Dārṣṭāntika reasoning to justify their claim. For them, the reflected images on a mirror "do not really exist" (*fei shi you* 非實有, MV T1545: 390c4), because the reflected object itself does not enter into the mirror. Echoes do not really exist because all sound is momentary, and one moment of sound cannot travel to produce a distant echo (MV T1545: 390c18–19). Dream-images do not really exist because we realize them being unreal upon awakening (MV T1545: 193b4–9). That magical creations (*nirmāṇa*) do not really exist is exactly because they are called magical creations (MV T1545: 696b25–29). When discussing these illusory objects, the Dārṣṭāntikas do not explicitly mention their concept of the cognition of nonexistent objects, but it is reasonable to assume that they would count on the nonexistence of these objects to argue for their concept of the cognition of nonexistent objects.

When discussing some other illusory objects, however, the Dārṣṭāntikas relate them to the mistaken cognition of self-view (*satkāyadṛṣṭi*), which, according to them, "has no real objects" (*wu shi suoyuan* 無實所緣). It is reported in MV:

> The Dārṣṭāntikas hold that self-view has no real objects. This is what they say: self-view conceptually constructs "I" and "mine." In the ultimate sense, however, there is no "I" or "mine." This is just like one cognizes a snake in place of a rope, or a human being in place of a pillar. Therefore, the self-view has no objects (*wu shuoyuan* 無所緣).[10]

Similar to the earlier case of "awareness without objects," the mistaken cognition without objects in the Dārṣṭāntika usage must also mean "the mistaken cognition of nonexistent objects." As I have pointed out in the previous chapter, the awareness of nonexistent objects is defined as the "awareness without objects" in the *Śāriputrābhidharma*. The two terms are often used interchangeably in some sources that mark the early development of this concept.

It requires sensory cognition to perceive illusory objects such as reflected images, echoes, shadow, mirage, fire-wheel, and magical creations. But to perceive a snake in place of a rope, a human being in place of a pillar, and, especially, a self in place of one's own body, it involves some more cognitive capacity than sensory perception. This is the capacity of conceptual construction that is attributed to mental consciousness. To cognize the latter group of illusory objects, sensory and mental consciousnesses must work together. On the other hand, with the possibility of cognizing both groups of illusory objects it proves that the cognition of nonexistent objects not only pertains to the level of sensory perception, but also to the level of mental cognition that involves conceptual construction. As compared to the early development of this concept, the Dārṣṭāntikas were innovative in bringing in illusory objects to argue for the cognition of nonexistent objects. The pervasive sensory and mental illusions provide rather strong support for this concept.

In his JP, Harivarman proposes seven arguments for the cognition of nonexistent objects. Among them, three are arguments from illusions and the other four are associated with meditation and negative judgments, which will be discussed in the following sections. First, he points out that "the illusory things produced [by magicians] are also nonexistent, but they are perceived as something existent."[11] For him, this phenomenon itself proves that "cognition also operates on the sphere of nonexistence."[12] He further singles out two particular cases of illusion: dreams and the optical illusion of double moon produced by pressing one's eyes. His opponent, in holding a Vaibhāṣika view that "the sphere upon which cognition operates is defined as the characteristic of existence,"[13] dismisses both cases as supportive examples for the cognition of nonexistent objects. In the case of double moon, the opponent thinks that it is because the subject does not perceive the moon carefully and the illusory second moon will disappear if she closes one of her eyes. Harivarman responds to this criticism by bringing up the case of patients with certain eye diseases who can see nonexistent hairs in front of them. In the case of dream, the opponent explains dream-images in terms of past experiences and external stimuli. Harivarman insists that some dream-images cannot be explained away by those factors and they would still support the idea that "there is the cognition that knows nonexistents."[14]

2.3 Negative Expressions

If the cognition of nonexistent objects involves the conceptual level, then a stronger support for this concept would be found in negative expressions and denials. Cox (1988: 45) refers to two passages in MV (T1545: 975a2ff, 42a20ff) that may suggest arguments from negative expressions and denials. Examining these passages carefully, however, I find that their relationship to our topic is rather weak because neither passage mentions the cognition of nonexistent objects or the Dārṣṭāntikas. In the latter passage, a question is raised with regard to the object of the negative statements that deny the existence of the unconditioned factors such as space and cessation without understanding (*apratisaṃkhyānirodha*). The answer is that "[the statements] just take as objects the names of space and cessation without understanding."[15] This reflects a standard Vaibhāṣika view that negative expressions and denials have their *existent* objects, that is, names, because names belong to the conditionings disassociated with mind (*citta-viprayukta-saṃskāra*) in their classification of existent factors. Moreover, just a few lines after the passage under discussion, names, or nominal existence (*ming you* 名有, **nāmasat*) is taken to be one of the five types of existence in one of their classification schemes of existence (MV T1545: 42a29). Hence, this passage from MV cannot be counted as evidence for the early Dārṣṭāntika argument for the cognition of nonexistent objects.

Explicit arguments from negative expressions for the cognition of nonexistent objects are found instead in Harivarman's JP. He quotes two Sūtra passages expressing the idea that at a certain stage a practitioner may observe her mental state and realize that she is devoid of desire (JP T1646: 254a6–7).

This negative statement on desire is counted as an argument for the cognition of nonexistent objects. In holding a Vaibhāṣika view, the opponent explains this negative statement in terms of the positive knowledge of reality, which is the state at which defilements such as desire are dispelled (JP T1646: 254b10–13). But Harivarman holds that the positive knowledge of reality and the negative knowledge of desire are not the same because the former bears a mark of impermanence, whereas the latter an illusory characteristic (JP T1646: 254c21–25).

2.4 Meditation of Nonexistent Objects

In their meditative practice, Buddhist practitioners are instructed to observe various different objects, which may vary depending on the type or stage of the meditative practice they are engaging in. Some of these meditative objects are mundane, but some are extraordinary. Now the question is: Do these extraordinary meditative objects exist? If they do not, how is it possible for a meditator to observe them?

In the *Śāriputrābhidharma*, an early Abhidharma work believed to be associated with the Mahīśāsakas and the Dharmaguptakas (Lü 1991: 1964–5), there is a long list of various types of meditation. Among these more than two hundred types of meditation, there is a meditation of nonexistent objects (*wu jingjie ding* 無境界定, **asadālambanasamādhi*) (T1548: 701c10–11). Later in the text, two definitions of this concept are given. The first presents some immediate problems: "What is meditation of nonexistent objects? There is no meditation of nonexistent objects."[16] In this literal translation, it sounds a denial of the very concept itself. This is counterintuitive, because this denial contradicts the fact that it is listed as one of more than two hundred types of meditation. I would rather make sense of this definition by interpolating a character *jing* (境; object); hence it would read: "What is meditation of nonexistent objects?

That which has no [objects] (alternatively, has nonexistents as [objects]) is the meditation of nonexistent objects."

My interpolation is not entirely arbitrary. Rather it is suggested in a similar definition of the awareness of nonexistent objects (*wu jingjie zhi* 無境界智, **asadālambanajñāna*). Some version of this definition reads: "What is awareness of nonexistent objects? There is no awareness of nonexistent objects."[17] But the Taishō version reads: "What is awareness of nonexistent objects? That which has no objects (alternatively, has nonexistents as objects) is the awareness of nonexistent objects."[18]

Some may notice that in both definitions there is an ambiguity between "that which has no objects" and "that which has nonexistents as objects." This ambiguity seems to prevail among many proponents of the cognition of nonexistent objects. In the previous chapter, I have examined a transition from an explicit denial of objects (*anārammaṇa*, *anālambana*) to an admission of negative entities as objects (*asadālambana*). These proponents seem to take advantage of this ambiguity and try to incorporate both meanings in their concept of the cognition of nonexistent objects. Saṃghabhadra, one of the most prominent Vaibhāṣika masters who argued fiercely against this concept, criticizes his opponent for being self-contradictory in doing so. He says:

> It is self-contradictory for him to say that there is the cognition (*buddhi*) of nonexistent objects. If cognition has objects, then he should not say that these objects are nonexistent; if objects are nonexistent, then he should not say that this cognition has objects. Since nonexistence means nothing altogether. If what he means is that the objects of this cognition themselves are nothing altogether, he should explicitly say that this cognition has no objects. Why does he act like a coward and deceive us by saying that there is cognition that takes nonexistents as objects? Therefore, there is definitely no cognition that takes nonexistents as objects.[19]

The second definition of the meditation of nonexistent objects reads: "Again, meditation arises when contemplating on past or future factors;

this is called meditation of nonexistent objects."[20] It is a shared strategy for the Dharmaguptakas, Uttarāpathakas, and later Dārṣṭāntika-Sautrāntikas to take the past and the future as nonexistent objects and use them as supportive cases for the cognition of nonexistent objects (see Chapter 1). But the early Dārṣṭāntikas as presented in MV do not share this view as they are still Sarvāstivādins, believing the existence of the past and the future. Now the Dharmaguptakas apply this view to the case of meditation, making a forceful argument for the meditation of nonexistent objects:

> There is meditation of past and future factors.
> Past and future factors do not exist.
> Therefore, there is meditation of nonexistent objects.

In Harivarman's JP, we see a further argument for the meditation of nonexistent objects with the support of a particular meditation. Harivarman proposes the following view: "Cognition also operates on the nonexistent sphere (*ākiṃcanyāyatana*). Why? Just like in resolving attention (*adhimuktimanaskāra*) one observes the blue in what is not blue . . . Because of the cognition of nonexistents, it is called the meditation that operates upon the nonexistent sphere."[21] Saṃghabhadra reports a similar view and attributes it to the Dārṣṭāntikas: "The Dārṣṭāntikas make such statements: . . . One must admit that nonexistents can also be objects and give rise to cognition . . . Because there is resolving attention that [observes its objects] as all-encompassing spheres. If all the cognitions have existent objects (lit., have objects), then there should be no resolving attention."[22]

In the Sarvāstivāda meditative tradition, three types of attention (*manaskāra*) are distinguished. The first is attention on particulars (*svalakṣaṇamanaskāra*) that observes the particular characteristics of certain objects, for example, earth as solid, water as wet, fire as warm, and wind as moving. The second is attention on universals (*sāmānyalakṣaṇamanaskāra*) that observes the general characteristics of objects, for example, the sixteen aspects of four noble truths. The third is resolving attention that is applied in such meditative practices as meditation on the loathsome, mindfulness of breathing, and visualization of all-encompassing spheres (*kṛtsnāyatana*).

The practice of observing the blue as mentioned by Harivarman is one example of the visualization of all-encompassing spheres. In such a practice, one has to embrace the object, for example, the blue color, exclusively and in its totality. Therefore, one not only observes the blue in what is actually blue, but also in what is not blue. The other all-encompassing spheres include the totality of earth, water, fire, and wind; yellow, red, and white; plus the uninterrupted spheres of space (*ākāśa*) and consciousness (*vijñāna*; see AKBh 8.36a, MV T1545: 440b11–12).

Both Harivarman and the Dārṣṭāntikas use the visualization of all-encompassing spheres as a supportive case for their concept of the cognition of nonexistent objects, because for them resolving attention is taking the nonexistent blue as objects. Saṃghabhadra argues against this view by explaining alternatively what is going on in this practice. He says: "Resolving attention should be understood accordingly this way. A yogic practitioner, having observed a small patch [of blue color], produces cognition with the aspect of totality through the power of his own resolution. This cognition is taking [existent] aggregates as objects."[23] The existent aggregates refer to the small patch of blue color that was observed at the beginning of the practice. Hence, according to Saṃghabhadra, the cognition still takes existent objects as objects, and it cannot be a case suggesting the cognition of nonexistent objects.

An opponent in JP offers another defense of this Sarvāstivāda view of Saṃghabhadra: "The quality of blue actually exists in things that are not [perceived as] blue. Just like a Sūtra says: 'The nature of purity exists in woods.'"[24] On this view, the quality or nature of blue that exists in non-blue things can serve as the object for the cognition of total and exclusive blue. Besides citing a Sūtra passage for support, the text, however, does not offer any further argument for this view.

The same opponent in JP tries to explain away the cognition of nonexistent objects by interpreting the seventh and eighth *dhyāna* differently. In response to Harivarman's using the seventh *dhyāna* as a supportive case for the cognition of nonexistent objects, the opponent says: "You said that because of the cognition of nonexistents it is called the meditation that operates upon the nonexistent sphere (*ākiṃcanyāyatana*). [But I think] this appearance of nonexistence is produced by the power of *samādhi* and itself is not nonexistent. Just like the existent matter can be destructed and appears as empty."[25] The opponent also thinks that in this stage of meditation, one does not observe nothing at all, instead he still observes a little something, which is so little that it can be conventionally called nothing. "Entering into this *samādhi*, one observes a little something that therefore can be called nothing. This is like [the conventions that] having a little salt can be called no salt and having a little wisdom can be called no wisdom."[26] With regard to the eighth *dhyāna*, the sphere of neither perception nor non-perception (*naivasaṃjñā-nāsaṃjñāyatana*), the opponent thinks that there is actually certain perception in this state, but for the same reason it is conventionally called neither perception nor non-perception.

For Harivarman, however, all these sophisms show nothing but the opponent's confusing and perverted views. He refutes them one by one:

> You said that [the blue existing in non-blue] is like the nature of purity existing in woods. It is not the case, because there would be the fault of the pre-existence of effects (*satkārya*) in causes. You also said that the mind cognizes certain blue color and turns it into the totality of [blue]. It is not the case either. There was originally a small patch of blue color, but now [you] observe all things on the earth as blue. This is a deluded view. Seeing a small patch of blue color, but observing the whole continent of Jambudvīpa as blue, isn't this a deluded view? . . . You said that the appearance of nonexistence is produced by the power of *samādhi* just like the existent matter can be destructed and appears as empty. If matter actually exists,

> but can be destructed into empty, then it is a perversion. Moreover, to call a little something nothing is also a perversion.[27]

Saṃghabhadra reports a similar accusation of perversion with regard to the meditation on the loathsome (*aśubhā*). "Some other masters said: . . . Since this meditation on the loathsome is encompassed by resolving attention, it should be reasonably called a perverted attention, and this meditation itself should not be good (*akuśala*). Not all its objects are skeletons, but it takes all of them as skeletons, isn't it a perversion?"[28] Saṃghabhadra responds to such a criticism by distinguishing two types of meditation on the loathsome. One is associated with attention on particulars (*svabhāvamanaskāra*). In this practice, the practitioner is instructed to observe the impurity of various parts of his own body: bones, flesh, blood, hair, and so on. Since this practice only observes what there really is and requires only attention on particulars, it does not involve perversion at all. However, Saṃghabhadra admits that this practice is not powerful enough to cut off our attachment to the impurities.

The other more powerful meditation on the loathsome is associated with resolving attention (*adhimuktimanaskāra*). In this practice, the practitioner first fixes her attention on a part of her body, either the toe, the forehead, or any other part; then she "purifies" the bone by removing the flesh, up to the point that she sees her entire body reduced to a skeleton. To increase the power of her resolving attention, she progressively creates the same idea of a second individual, of individuals of the monastery, of the village, of the country, up to the whole earth, as being filled with skeletons (see AKBh 6.10a–b). Saṃghabhadra admits that this visualization involves imaginations that do not necessarily see things as they are, but it is still not perverted attention, because it is powerful enough to eliminate defilements. He analyzes this visualization in a peculiar way:

> This is what the practitioner thought: "Although the object-field is not filled with skeletons, for the purpose of taming defilements, I shall visualize with resolution that it is filled with skeletons." Since it can tame defilements and

> fulfill her will of liberation, how can it be a perversion? The power of this visualization can tame and conceal defilements. Having such skillful power, how can it be no good? Therefore, it does not have the fault [of perversion] as accused.[29]

Here Saṃghabhadra adopts a pragmatic theory of truth: anything useful to the final liberation is good, non-perversive, and true. This may help him win the debate with his opponent, but it seems to have deviated from the usual Buddhist claim of knowing reality as it is.

Interestingly enough, long before the debates of Harivarman with his opponent and Saṃghabhadra with the Dārṣṭāntikas, there was a similar debate on the same topic between the Theravādins and their opponent Andhakas, a Mahāsāṃghika sub-group. In their debate, the focal point comes back to the visualization of all-encompassing spheres (*kasiṇāyatana*), now using earth rather than blue as example. Their controversial point is: "For someone who has achieved the meditative attainment (*samāpatti*) of all-encompassing earth, is her cognition perverted?"[30] Same as the Sarvāstivādins, the Theravādins also recognize ten all-encompassing spheres, but they replace the last one, "consciousness" (*vijñāna*), with "bright light" (*āloka*). In the practice of all-encompassing earth, the practitioner is also instructed to observe earth exclusively and in its totality. Gradually she should be able to see earth everywhere. Now the Andhakas ask: "For someone who has achieved [the meditative attainment of all-encompassing] earth, does everything become earth?"[31] Anyone with a commonsensical mind, including the Theravādins, would answer no, because the all-encompassing earth can exist only in the practitioner's imaginary visualization, not in reality. The Andhakas conclude that exactly because of this it is a perverted cognition for someone who sees the all-encompassing earth everywhere.

In a footnote of their English translation of the *Kathāvatthu*, Shwe and Davids (1969 [*c.* 1915]: 176 n3) criticize some contemporary Burmese Buddhists for their serious practice of earth-gazing to achieve a state "when every external thing seems to become earth," and consider this state as "true hallucination." It seems that we are facing a dilemma here. If one takes seriously the visualization of all-encompassing spheres, she is engaging a self-induced hallucination; if what happens in this practice is not taken to be true, then this practice itself is perverted as it does not observe reality as it is.

The Theravāda refutations to the Andhakas' position further elaborate this dilemma. On the one hand, the visualization of all-encompassing spheres is one of the most important practices in the Buddhist tradition, and those who have achieved it are highly regarded. On the other hand, it does resemble those "real" perversions that see the permanent in the impermanent, happiness in ill, a soul in what is not soul, the beautiful in the ugly. Their refutations are proved ineffective, and the Theravāda view on the issue remains inconclusive.

In his commentary on the *Kathāvatthu*, Buddhaghosa spells out more clearly the Theravāda view. First of all, he distinguishes the concept of earth from earth itself, and holds that "the concept (*nimitta*) which arises by means of earth is not earth itself."[32] For him, "earth" can have various different meanings. "The term 'earth' may mean the quality of earth (*lakkhaṇapaṭhavī*), physical earth (*saṃbhārapaṭhavī*), the concept of earth (*nimittapaṭhavī*), or the earth-god (*paṭhavīdevatā*)."[33] Therefore, in the current case, if one confuses the all-encompassing earth with the earth itself, then his cognition is perverted; if, however, he takes it as a concept or percept (*sañña*) of earth, then there is no perversion at all. With this conceptualist approach, Buddhaghosa has developed a rather sensible view on this controversial issue.

2.5 Four Arguments

Based on scattered sources from MV, JP, and NA, we have reconstructed four arguments for the cognition of nonexistent objects that are attributed to the Dārṣṭāntikas. The first argument from conjunction and feeling is similar to the Mahāsāṃghika argument from latent defilements as both focus on the emotional aspect of human mind. The Dārṣṭāntikas disagree with the Sarvāstivāda view that both conjunction and its objects are real existence. They hold that conjunction is real, but its objects do not exist as real entities. The objects of conjunction are distinguished from the physical objects of perception. The former is called "internal things," which are objects of mental feeling, whereas the latter is "external things," which serve as objects of bodily feeling. By denying the existence of these internal things, the Dārṣṭāntikas establish the cognition of nonexistent objects with respect to conjunction and mental feeling.

The second argument from illusions is a Dārṣṭāntika innovation that was influential among later Dārṣṭāntika-Sautrāntikas. The great variety of illusions that we can easily experience in daily life provides strong support for this argument. Some illusions, for example, reflected images, shadow, mirage, fire-wheel, and magical creations, are perceived by sensory cognition as they are merely optical illusions. Some other illusions, for example, perceiving a snake in place of a rope, a human being in place of a pillar, and, especially, a self in place of one's own body, involve both sensory and mental cognition as they are mentally constructed illusions. Both groups of illusions are considered as nonexistent; the very fact that we can perceive or cognize them proves that there is the cognition of nonexistent objects.

The third argument from negative expressions is found in Harivarman's JP. For him, the state when a practitioner realizes that she is devoid of desire is counted as a supportive case for the cognition of nonexistent objects. The opponent explains this negative statement on desire in terms of the positive knowledge of reality, which is described as a state when desire is expelled. But Harivarman holds that the two are different as the positive state is impermanent, whereas the negative state is illusory.

The fourth argument from meditative objects involves some scattered sources on the ontological status of meditative objects in such practices as the visualization of all-encompassing spheres and the meditation on the loathsome. I have discussed the related debates on this topic between the Theravādins and the Andhakas, Harivarman and his opponent, Saṃghabhadra, and the Dārṣṭāntikas. One way to characterize these debates is to divide them into two camps. One camp is represented by Saṃghabhadra, Harivarman's opponent, and possibly the Theravādins. They advocate a view of realism: these meditative objects are real *existent* objects. The other camp is represented by Harivarman, the Dārṣṭāntikas, the Andhakas, and the Dharmaguptakas. They hold a view of antirealism in this particular case: these meditative objects are *nonexistent* objects, and those who take them to be existent are perverted. These two treads of metaphysical thinking have been engaging in debates throughout the history of philosophy, but neither of them ever claimed final victory. This is also the situation we see in the debates in this chapter that involves quite a few Buddhist philosophical schools. Conceptualism, the middle way between these two extremes, seems not so popular among these early Buddhist philosophers except for Buddhaghosa, who clearly advocates such a position. In the history of Western philosophy, it is this middle position that gets popular support. Among Buddhist philosophers, we only find that conceptualism becomes a viable option through the efforts of the Yogācāras and Buddhist logicians (see Chapter 6).

3

Yogācāra

In this chapter, I will focus on the arguments developed by Yogācāra Buddhists in support of the knowability of nonexistents and evaluate how successfully they have established their view that one can know what there is not. The sources that I am going to deal with are some sections of the encyclopedic *Yogācārabhūmi* (YBh) that discuss the concepts of the cognition (*buddhi*) of nonexistent objects or the consciousness (*vijñāna*) of nonexistent objects.

3.1 "Mental Consciousness Takes Nonexistents as Objects"

Before examining these arguments, we should formulate the thesis that they are attempting to prove. However, this turns out to be not an easy task. The shorter first section (text A) under discussion is from the most ancient layer of YBh. In this section, the key point is to establish the concept of the cognition of nonexistent objects with a major and a minor argument, but it does not explain what this cognition (*buddhi*) is. Nor does it explicitly state the thesis they try to prove. The second, longer section (text B) under discussion is from the *Viniścayasaṃgrahanī* section of YBh, which is apparently a commentary and elaboration on text A. In this section, two major and five minor arguments are developed to prove the following thesis:

> Thesis 1: "Therefore, it is known that there is the mental consciousness (*yishi* 意識, *yid kyi rnam par shes pa*) that takes nonexistents as objects."[1]

Here, the key concept is the mental consciousness of nonexistent objects. Elsewhere, a similar thesis is stated: "Hence we know that mental consciousness in the same way takes nonexistents as objects."[2] The Tibetan translation, however, simply has "*yid*" (mind, mental) instead of "*yid kyi rnam par shes pa*" (mental consciousness).[3] In the established Yogācāra doctrinal system, mind (*manas*) and mental consciousness (*manovijñāna*) become two distinctive concepts. But in the earlier Yogācāra and Abhidharma sources, mind (*manas*, *yi*,意, *yid*) is normally used in the way that covers both the sense of mental organ (*manas*) and mental consciousness (*manovijñāna*). As the passage under discussion is drawn from the early Yogācāra work YBh, it is therefore justified to interpolate "consciousness" (*shi* 識), as Xuanzang (玄奘) did in his Chinese translation. So the two statements express the same idea: mental consciousness takes nonexistents as objects.

In another concluding remark, there seems to be a different thesis stated:

> Thesis 2: "One should also know that there are further rational discourses of a similar kind that fully establish the consciousness (*shi*識, *rnam par shes pa*) of nonexistent objects."[4]

Here the more general term "consciousness" (*vijñāna*) instead of the specific "mental consciousness" is used. In an alternative Chinese translation of the *Viniścayasaṃgrahanī* by Paramārtha, it is stated even more explicitly as follows: "For this reason, it is definitely known that all consciousnesses (*zhu shi* 諸識) take nonexistents as objects."[5] The term "consciousness" or "all consciousnesses" covers not only mental consciousness, but also the five sense consciousnesses, which, in the Indian philosophical tradition, refer to visual, auditory, olfactory, gustatory, and tactile sensations. Does this mean that the Yogācāras try to prove that visual and auditory consciousnesses can also take nonexistents as objects? Do they believe that we can actually see or hear nonexistents? If so, they would have a much greater theoretical burden than simply proving the mental consciousness of nonexistent objects.

In Paramārtha's translation, a brief dialogue is inserted by Paramārtha to explain this point. A question is raised: "If visual consciousness cannot take nonexistents as objects, how can mental consciousness (*xinshi* 心識, **manovijñāna*) take nonexistents as objects?"[6] Here, the opponent explicitly denies the possibility of having visual consciousness of nonexistent objects, and in turn questions the proponent's thesis of the mental consciousness of nonexistent objects. In his reply, the proponent does not object to the denial of the visual consciousness of nonexistent objects. He simply states that mental consciousness can take nonexistents as objects because it can penetrate objects of all three times, namely, the past, present, and future.

Based on both Paramārtha's and Xuanzang's translations, we can safely assume that Thesis 2 is not intended to establish the sense consciousness of nonexistent objects. Instead, it is only meant to express a more general concept of the consciousness of nonexistent objects, which, in the same way as the concept of the awareness of nonexistent objects implies, only refers to the more specific mental consciousness of nonexistent objects. So we can treat both Theses 1 and 2 as proving the same view: mental consciousness takes nonexistents as objects. In other words, the Yogācāras try to prove that one can think or know nonexistents, but not see or hear them.

3.2 The Past and the Future

As mentioned earlier, there is one major and one minor argument in text A and two major and five minor arguments in text B. For our analysis, I will group them into five major arguments. Among them, the first argument deals with the past and the future. The Yogācāra and Sautrāntika concepts of the cognition of nonexistent objects were developed against the backdrop of the Sarvāstivādins' epistemological argument for the existence of the past and the future. This epistemological argument can be formulated in the following simple way:

1 Whatever is knowable is existent.
2 The past and the future are knowable.
3 Therefore, the past and the future exist.

However, the Yogācāras and other major Buddhist philosophical schools committed themselves to a view of presentism, that is, only the present exists; the past and the future do not. Under their view of presentism, the Yogācāras would surely reject the conclusion. However, they accept premise 2, and, in turn, they would have to reject premise 1. By formulating the Yogācāra view against the existence of the past and the future, we arrive at their argument for the cognition of nonexistent objects:

1 Mental consciousness can know past and future objects.
2 Things in the past or the future do not exist.
3 Therefore, mental consciousness can know nonexistent objects.

For someone committed to presentism, premise 2 is unproblematic. The contentious statement is premise 1. To support premise 1, the Yogācāras came up with the following argument: "Because it is evident that mental consciousness takes the past and the future consciousnesses (*shi* 識, *rnam par shes pa*) as objects."[7] A *sūtra* passage quoted in text B also supports this argument by saying: "Depending on the past phenomena (*saṃskāra*), there arises mind (*manas*); depending on the future phenomena, there arises mind."[8] In other words, the argument is that mental consciousness, or mind, can take the past and the future consciousnesses or phenomena as objects, and since objects of the past and the future are under the purview of past and future consciousnesses, they become objects of the present mental consciousness as well. The key to understanding this point is that mental consciousness is believed to be able to penetrate objects of all the three times, that is, past, present, and future, even though the five sense consciousnesses can only take their respective present objects as objects.

The second key point to be kept in mind is that the objects of mental consciousness are believed to comprise *all* dharmas.[9] What are all *dharmas*? Text A refers to a presumably Abhidharma view that holds: "All [*dharmas*] etc. refer only to the twelve sense spheres (*āyatana*)."[10] The twelve sense spheres include five sense organs (eye, ear, nose, tongue, and body) and their respective objects (form, sound, smell, taste, and tangible things) plus mind and its object *dharma*. These twelve sense spheres are believed to be the basic elements (*dharma*) from which the whole phenomenal world is built. The phenomenal world can be considered illusory because of its compounded and finite nature, but its building blocks are real existents. In the same passage, the existence of all these *dharmas* is emphasized: "All *existents* (*sarvam asti*) etc. refer only to the twelve sense spheres."[11] This traditional Abhidharma view takes the object of mental consciousness ("all *dharmas*") to be the twelve sense spheres, which cover all the real existents. Therefore, we should take "*dharma*" here to mean "real existents." If this is the case, then past and future consciousnesses, as mentioned in the supportive argument of the Yogācāras, are apparently not included in the twelve sense spheres, so they are examples of nonexistent objects. Past or future consciousnesses here are considered to be nonexistent probably because they are *of* the past or the future, for the same reason that we would consider all the past or the future phenomena as nonexistents.

However, it is self-contradictory to say that the objects of mental consciousness, which are real existent (*dharmas*), are nonexistent. The Yogācāras think that the problem is due to a narrow understanding of the term "*dharma*" as "real existents" alone. They believe that there is a hidden meaning of the Buddha, according to which "mind can grasp whatever object (*don gang*) that is not the object-field (*gocara*) of five [sense] consciousnesses, which is metaphorically designated as *dharma* by the Buddha."[12] In other words, mental consciousness not only takes as objects the *dharma* as sense spheres (*fachu* 法處, *chos kyi skye mched*) or real existents, but also whatever that is beyond the object-field of five sense consciousnesses, which is the designated or conceptual *dharma* (*jiashuo ming fa* 假說名法, *chos gdags pa*). Although the past and the future consciousnesses are not real existents as the sense spheres are, they are designated or conceptual *dharmas*; therefore they can be the objects of mental consciousness. The same applies to all the past and the future phenomena. In his commentary on YBh, Kuiji adds that even the "sky-flower," an extreme case of a nonexistent object, can be designated as a *dharma* and be cognized by mental consciousness.[13] This implies that he takes the designated or conceptual *dharmas* as nonexistent objects.

If the notion of *dharma* is expanded to cover not only the *dharmas* as sense spheres, that is, real existents, but also the designated *dharma*, or nonexistents, then it would not be self-contradictory to say that the objects of mental consciousness (i.e., *dharmas*) can be nonexistent. However, we are then confronted with another problem. If *dharma* includes both existents and nonexistents within itself, then what is this *dharma*? This issue is addressed in the second argument.

3.3 Existents and Nonexistents

The second argument is based on a radically new interpretation of the concept of *dharma* proposed by the Yogācāras. According to them, *dharma* is derived from the verbal root √*dhṛ*, literally meaning "to hold, bear, or maintain." Hence, an existent *dharma* means something that bears the characteristics of existence; similarly, a nonexistent *dharma* means something that bears the characteristics of nonexistence. Both existence and nonexistence are therefore included in the notion of *dharma*. "*Dharmas* with the characteristics of existence bear the characteristics of existence; *dharma*s with the characteristics of nonexistence bear the characteristics of nonexistence. Hence [both existence and nonexistence] are called *dharma*."[14] In other words, *dharma* can be understood literally as something held in mind, the knowable, or as a potential intentional object. As we have discussed earlier, this concept is more fundamental than such concepts as existence or nonexistence, being or nonbeing. The prevailing understanding and interpretation of *dharma* in terms of existents, or elements of existence, was posited by the dominant Sarvāstivāda ontology, which expels nonexistence or nonbeing from its realm and suggests that only that which exists is knowable. The Yogācāras argue against this dominant view by establishing the cognition of nonexistent objects. Their arguments can be analyzed in three steps. The first step is:

> **1** "With regard to existents (*youxing* 有性, *yod pa*), one can establish existent objects and grasp existent objects; with regard to nonexistents (*wuxing* 無性, *med pa*), one can establish nonexistent objects and grasp nonexistent objects."[15]

Rephrasing this in contemporary philosophical terms, we may say: with regard to what there is, we can establish existent objects and take them to be intentional existent objects; with regard to what there is not, we can establish nonexistent objects and take them to be intentional nonexistent objects. This way both existent and nonexistent objects are established, and they are both taken to be intentional objects.

The second step is concerned with the subjective side:

> **2** "Because mental consciousness, with regard to existents, if it can establish a certain [existent] object, then it can cognize this very [existent] object; with regard to nonexistents, if it can establish a certain [nonexistent] object, then it can cognize this very [nonexistent] object."[16]

Here it is clear that on the subjective side, mental consciousness is responsible for and is capable of cognizing both existent and nonexistent objects. If it can intend a certain existent object, it can cognize this very existent object; if it can intend a certain nonexistent object, it can cognize this very nonexistent object. In other words, intention presupposes cognition.

After discussing both the objective and subjective aspects of the issue, the Yogācāras conclude their second argument with the third step:

> **3** "If the two kinds [of mental consciousness] do not cognize these two kinds of [existent and nonexistent] objects, then it is unreasonable to say that mind can take all objects as objects and grasp all objects."[17]

The two kinds of mental consciousness refer to those that cognize existent and nonexistent objects respectively. They belong to one and the same mental consciousness. If this mental consciousness can cognize only existent but not nonexistent objects, then it should not be said that mental consciousness takes all *dharmas* as objects. By reinterpreting *dharmas* more broadly as intentional objects, the Yogācāras establish their concept of the cognition of nonexistent objects. This view does not violate the doctrine that mental consciousness takes all *dharmas* as objects, which is accepted by all the major Buddhist philosophical schools.

One might question whether the three steps in this line of reasoning clearly constitute a valid argument. Let me reformulate this argument in the following five steps:

> **1** Mental consciousness takes all *dharmas* as intentional objects.
> **2** All *dharmas* include both existent and nonexistent objects.
> **3** Therefore, mental consciousness takes both existent and nonexistent objects as intentional objects.

4 Intention presupposes cognition.

5 Therefore, mental consciousness can know both existent and nonexistent objects.

In this reformulation, premise 1 restates what is implied in step 3, a commonly accepted thesis in Buddhism. Premise 2 is a reformulation of step 1. Premise 3 is drawn from 1 and 2. Premise 4 is the central idea of step 2. Finally, we arrive at the conclusion, step 5, with an apparently valid argument.

Moreover, yogic practice is invoked in text A to explain this argument. "If otherwise, that is, the yogic practitioners only know existents but do not know nonexistents, then they should not be those who intimately observe the *dharmas* as objects. But this is unreasonable."[18] Text A also refers to a *sūtra* passage to support this view: "Again the World-honored One said: 'My disciple of non-deceit, as I have taught, the correct practice is that with regard to existents, one knows existents, and that with regard to nonexistents, one knows nonexistents.'"[19] This quotation shows that not only in theory, but also in practice, the Yogācāras should know both existents and nonexistents through their mental consciousness. Otherwise, they are not carrying out the correct practice, nor do they correctly observe the *dharmas* as objects.

3.4 No-Self and Impermanence

We have seen that the first argument concerns the past and the future and the second argument deals with existents and nonexistents. In text A, there is a brief discussion on no-self, which can be formulated as the third argument. The text says:

> If it [i.e., the cognition that grasps nonexistents] does not arise, then there would not be the cognition (*buddhi*) that grasps no-self, the horn of a rabbit, the son of a barren woman, etc. But this is unreasonable.[20]

In text B, after presenting the main arguments that we have analyzed as arguments 1 and 2 earlier, five additional arguments, which are called the five rational discourses of *vaipulya* (*guangda* 廣大, *yangs shing rgya che ba*), are introduced.[21] The first and fourth rational discourses of *vaipulya* are related to the topic of no-self:

> **1** As the Buddha has elegantly said, "There is no-self inside, outside and in between the two." This selflessness is not included in the conditioned [*dharmas*], nor is it included in the unconditioned [*dharmas*]. Regarding the conceptual cognition (*yongs su rtog pa*, **parikalpa*) of universals (*sāmānyalakṣaṇa*), it is not the case that the consciousness of this object [of selflessness] does not arise.[22] This is the first rational discourse.[23]
>
> **2** Again, all phenomena (*saṃskāra*) are not permanent, stable or eternal. The very nature (*xing* 性, *nyid*) of impermanence, unstableness and the non-eternality of all phenomena is not included in the conditioned [*dharmas*], nor is it included in the unconditioned [*dharmas*]. Regarding the conceptual cognition of universals, it is not the case that the consciousness of this object [of the very nature of impermanence, unstableness, and non-eternality] does not arise.[24] . . . This is the fourth rational discourse.[25]

All these arguments rely heavily on the concepts of no-self and impermanence, two foundational Buddhist teachings. Both concepts can be rephrased into negative judgments: "The substantial self (*ātman*) does not exist," and "The permanent entity does not exist." The key to understanding this set of arguments lies in the relationship between linguistic and logical negation and the ontological nonexistence. In other words, the issue being addressed here is whether or not negative judgments have to be based on an ontological commitment to nonexistence. If they do, it is easier to explain negation and any kind of negative cognition, but there is a danger of reifying a nonexistent object or entity, which sounds like a self-contradictory concept. If they don't, we do not have to multiply unnecessary entities, and can limit negation and negative cognition to the scope of language or cognition. But this way, negation and negative cognitions become only secondary and derivative as compared to affirmation and positive cognitions. The second option seems to be popular among Western philosophers, who tend to avoid the ontological commitment to nonexistence and try to limit negation and negative cognitions to the scope of language and cognition (Horn 1989: 45–79). The Yogācāras seem to favor the first option and believe that negative judgments associated with no-self or impermanence are based on an ontological commitment to selflessness or the very nature of impermanence. Because there is no self in the first place, we can then say that "there is no self" and derive a concept of no-self. Because all phenomena are impermanent in reality, we can then state that "all phenomena are impermanent" and have a concept of impermanence.

What, then, is the ontological status of this selflessness and the very nature of impermanence? The Yogācāras say that they are not included in either conditioned or unconditioned *dharma*s. In the metaphysical framework that is accepted or presumed by the major Buddhist philosophical schools, there are two basic types of *dharma*s or existents. One is the conditioned existents that are governed by causal relations, which comprise material form (*rūpa*), mind (*citta*), mental activities (*caitta*), and the elements that are neither material nor mental (*cittaviprayuktasaṃskāra*). The other is the unconditioned existents that go beyond causal relations; this class of things mainly consists of *nirvāṇa*, the final goal of all Buddhist practices. Different Buddhist schools developed various schemes to classify these main types of existents, but none of them would include selflessness in their classification of existents. So selflessness should be similar to the case of the horn of a rabbit or the son of a barren woman and be classified as a nonexistent. The same applies to impermanence. In his commentary to YBh, Dunnyun (遁倫) confirms this point by quoting a definition from the *Bodhisattvabhūmi* (BBh) section of YBh, which says: "Here the conditioned and unconditioned [*dharmas*] are called existents; self (*ātmā*) or mine (*ātmīya*) are called nonexistents."[26]

Having made it clear that selflessness and the very nature of impermanence enjoy the ontological status of nonexistence, the Yogācāras move on to their subjective aspect. With what kind of cognition can one cognize selflessness or impermanence? The Tibetan translation states: "Regarding the conceptual cognition of universals, it is not the case that the consciousness of this object [of selflessness] does not arise" (YBht, D4038: zhi17a6–7). Xuanzang's Chinese translation conflates "cognition" with "consciousness" and reads: "The consciousness of universals does not arise without taking this object [of selflessness] as object" (YBhc, T1579: 585 a11–12). So it is the conceptual cognition (**parikalpa*) or consciousness (*vijñāna*) of universals (*sāmānyalakṣaṇa*) that is responsible for the cognition of selflessness. In his commentary to YBh, Dunnyun quotes a view attributed to his contemporary Huijing (惠景), who explained the observation of no-self, or impermanence, in three different stages. In the stages of learning and thinking, one observes no-self or impermanence as abstract universals through inference (*anumāna*). In the further stage of practice, one is supposed to observe the particular characteristics of no-self or impermanence through direct realization (*abhisamaya*), which is a cognition or perception (*pratyakṣa*) of particulars (*svalakṣaṇa*). But in YBh, the observation of no-self or impermanence is called the cognition of universals, regardless of the different stages of learning, thinking, and practice. Why is this? Dunnyun quotes again Huijing's views to explain this discrepancy. One view holds that although in reality the cognition of no-self in the stage of practice is a cognition of particulars, it is convenient to call it the cognition of universals despite its appearance in different stages. However, this reasoning of convenience is not convincing. Another argument holds that although particular objects (*zixiang jingjie* 自相境界) are observed in the stage of practice, these particular objects can be called universals because each individual phenomenon is no-self and impermanent, and hence all phenomena are universally no-self and impermanent. Each particular is a manifestation of the universal. Therefore, even the observation of no-self in the stage of practice can be called a cognition of universals.[27]

Even with this discrepancy, the strength of the current argument is not weakened. Although the observation of no-self and impermanence in the stage of practice can be considered a cognition of particulars, hence a perception, it is not a regular type of sense perception like seeing or hearing, but rather a yogic perception, which is still a capacity of mental consciousness rather than sense consciousness.[28] In the stages of learning and thinking, the cognition of no-self and impermanence is attributed to inference, which is surely a capacity of mental consciousness. So both cases would support the thesis to be proved: mental consciousness can cognize nonexistent objects such as selflessness and impermanence.

3.5 Food and Drinks

The fourth argument corresponds to the second rational discourse of *vaipulya* and is concerned with food and drinks, which are assumed to be not really existent according to major Buddhist schools. It is stated in text B:

> Again, food, drinks, vehicles, clothes, ornaments, house, army, and forest etc. are metaphorically designated upon the bases of form, smell, taste and tangible things, which arise, change and are established this and that way. These food and drinks etc. do not exist at all apart from form and smell etc. Their very nature of nonexistence (*wu you xing* 無有性, *med pa nyid*) is not included in the conditioned [*dharmas*], nor is it included in the unconditioned [*dharmas*]. Regarding the cognition of particulars, it is not the case that the consciousness of this object [of the very nature of nonexistence] does not arise.[29] This is the second rational discourse.[30]

To make sense of this argument, we have to understand the nominalist position that was accepted or presumed among major Buddhist philosophical schools. According to this received view, the real existents are the five classes of conditioned and unconditioned *dharma*s that we have mentioned in the previous section. Form, smell, taste, and what is tangible are covered in the class of material form (*rūpa*), which also includes the rest of the six elements, that is, sound and the five senses (eye, ear, nose, tongue, and body).[31] In other words, this view assigns existence to the constituents of sensible objects and physical organs alone. The entire material world is built upon these basic elements. They arise, combine, change, and are sustained in various different ways, which produce the colorful world that we experience. This picture is rather similar to the worldview as advocated by contemporary scientific realism, which takes the fundamental reality of the material world to be the interactions between various particles and basic forces. As a matter of fact, the Buddhists and the scientific realists shared the common heritage of atomism as developed in both ancient India and Greece.

Under this atomistic realism, food and drinks are said not to exist at all apart from form and smell, because they are metaphorically designated upon the bases of these existent elements. Food and drinks are called universals, whereas form and smell are particulars. Now do these universals exist or not? There are two existing views. One is to take them to exist in the manner of designated or conceptual existents (*prajñaptisat*), and this is the view of the Sarvāstivādins. The other holds that they do not exist precisely because they are designated and conceptual, and this view was advocated by the Sautrāntikas. In this context of discussing the cognition of nonexistent objects, the Yogācāras seem to adopt the latter view, as they hold that food and drinks, being nonexistents, are not included in the categories of either conditioned or unconditioned existents. In his commentary to the *Nyāyapraveśa*, a work of Buddhist logic, Kuiji states that "if [universals] exist, then this would disprove the cognition of nonexistent objects."[32] For Kuiji, universals do not exist, and one knows universals through his or her conceptual cognition, hence there is the cognition of nonexistent objects. If, however, universals exist, then the knowledge of universals only proves the cognition of *existent* rather than nonexistent objects. This implies that the Yogācāras have to treat universals as nonexistents if they accept the cognition of nonexistent objects.

Nonetheless, the Yogācāras still conceive the possibility of cognizing food and drinks. What kind of cognition is involved with nonexistent food and drinks? Text B says that it is the cognition or consciousness of particulars. This is problematic because food and drinks are universals, rather than particulars. Moreover, the cognition of particulars would be a sense perception; for instance, visual perception can perceive an existent visual object, but not nonexistent food or drinks. Kuiji tries to explain away the problem by insisting that the particulars here are not the objects of sense perception, nor are they in contrast to universals; instead, they only refer to food and drinks *themselves*.[33] The cognition of the nonexistent food and drinks themselves is therefore not sense perception, and it is still the function of *mental consciousness*. The alternative Chinese translation by Paramārtha simply takes it to be the cognition of universals (*zongxiang* 総相, **sāmānyalakṣaṇa*),[34] which is also the function of mental consciousness. Without the Sanskrit original, we cannot determine which solution is justified. But in either case, it would support the thesis to be proved: mental consciousness can cognize the nonexistent objects, such as food and drinks.

3.6 Heretical Views

The fifth and final argument corresponds to the third rational discourse of *vaipulya* and is concerned with the heretical view of nihilism.[35] It is stated in text B:

> Again, the heretical view of the nihilists holds that there is no donation, no wish, and no worship . . . Suppose that the very nature of the nonexistence of

donation, wish, worship etc. really is an existent,[36] then such views as [that there exist soul (*puruṣa*) and person (*pudgala*)][37] would not be heretical views. Why?[38] Because it would be a correct view and a correct assertion. But if [their very nature of nonexistence] does not exist, for those who hold heretical views, their consciousness of such an object would not arise.[39] This is the third rational discourse.[40]

The heretical view under discussion is labeled nihilism. In the eyes of its opponents in the Indian tradition, Buddhism is often viewed as a school of nihilism that negates everything. Major Buddhist philosophical schools, however, try to maintain a "middle way" position that goes beyond the extremes of nihilism and eternalism. In the context of discussing the cognition of nonexistent objects, it is especially important for Buddhist philosophers to distance themselves from nihilism, because the ontological commitment to nonexistent objects can easily lead to the impression of opponents that Buddhism really does represent an extreme form of nihilism.

The heretical views are said to deny donation, wish, and worship, which sounds like a kind of ethical or religious version of nihilism. These views are extensively discussed and refuted elsewhere in YBh, where it points out that ethical or religious nihilism is based on a metaphysical nihilism, which claims that "all things with all characteristics do not exist."[41] If Buddhism also holds that all these things really do not exist, then the nihilists who hold that they do not exist would be expressing a correct but not heretical view.

On the Yogācāra view, however, it is not the case that all things do not exist. Some things exist, some things do not. A correct cognition consists of two aspects: the cognition of existents as existents, and the cognition of nonexistents as nonexistents. The nihilists, according to the Yogācāras, made a mistake by taking existents as nonexistents. Since donation, wish, and worship do exist, there would not arise any cognition of their nonexistence. If the nihilists still believe that they do not exist, they hold a wrong and heretical view.

From this reasoning, we can infer that the difference between the correct and wrong views lies in their correspondence to reality, and that the Yogācāras here would embrace a correspondence theory of truth. A correct view of existents corresponds to relevant existent objects, and a correct view of nonexistents corresponds to relevant nonexistent objects. In contrast, a wrong view of either existents or nonexistents does not have a corresponding existent or nonexistent object. So the cognition of nonexistent objects that the Yogācāras try to prove here would be a correct view. Accordingly, a cognition of nonexistents without corresponding nonexistent objects as advocated by the nihilists would be a wrong view.

3.7 Five Arguments

In this chapter, I have examined each of the five Yogācāra arguments for the cognition of nonexistent objects in their historical context. Now let us evaluate how successful these arguments are for the purpose of establishing the view that one can know what there is not. In the history of philosophy, this view is also called an object view of intentionality. The main rival of the object view is the existent-object view, which is the view shared by Parmenides, Vaiśeṣikas, Sarvāstivādins, and many other Western and Eastern philosophers. On this view, all the knowables, or potential intentional objects, are existent objects, either in the forms of abstracta, mental concreta, or possibilita, depending on different versions of this theory to which one may subscribe. To argue against this dominant view, the main agenda of the object view is to introduce and establish the concept of the cognition of nonexistent objects. This approach also distances itself from a more recent but popular rival—the adverbialist theory of intentionality, which tends to rid philosophical discourse of intentional objects altogether, either of the existent or nonexistent variety.[42]

There are two logical steps to establish the cognition of nonexistent objects. First, nonexistents are *the objects of cognition*; second, these objects of cognition are *nonexistents*. On the first step, the Yogācāras had repeatedly made it clear that mental consciousness can take as objects nonexistent objects (argument 2), the past and the future (argument 1), no-self and impermanence (argument 3), and universals such as food and drinks (argument 4). Regardless of the variety of these objects, they are all unproblematically objects of mental consciousness.

Now on the second step, we can use the popular fourfold classification of nonbeing or nonexistence (*abhāva*) among Indian philosophers as a benchmark. In argument 2, the general concept of nonexistent objects is contrasted to existent objects. In argument 1, the past and the future correspond respectively to two basic types of nonexistence, specifically, posterior nonexistence (*dhvaṃsa*), that is, the nonexistence of something after it has ceased to exist, and prior nonexistence (*prāgabhāva*), the nonexistence of something before it has come into existence. In argument 3, no-self and impermanence are treated on a par with such things as the horn of a rabbit and the son of a barren woman, two famous examples of the third type of nonexistence—absolute nonexistence (*atyantābhāva*). In argument 4, universals such as food and drinks are taken to be nonexistents. However, they do not directly correspond to the final type of nonexistence—mutual nonexistence (*anyonyābhāva*). In argument 5, the Yogācāras argue for a general object view of intentionality and distance themselves from a heretical view without corresponding objects, which can be seen as a version of the adverbialist theory of intentionality.

Therefore, I conclude that the Yogācāras have, to a great extent, successfully established their concept of the cognition of nonexistent objects, and strengthened the object view of intentionality against its rivals.

4

Vasubandhu

In Chapter 1, I traced the origin of the concept of the cognition of nonexistent objects to the earliest available Buddhist sources and to the earliest Buddhist school of Mahāsāṃghika and its sub-schools. In Chapter 3, I examined some early texts of the Yogācāra school that argue for the validity of this concept. In between Mahāsāṃghika and Yogācāra, there was the well-known controversy on this very issue between two sectarian schools of Sarvāstivāda and Dārṣṭāntika-Sautrāntika. It has been studied in some detail by La Vallée Poussin (1936–37), Sakamoto (1981: 135–56), Yoshimoto (1982: 146–56), Cox (1988), Dhammajoti (2007a: 44–8), and Kwan (2007). Most of these studies, however, treat the numerous texts and figures concerned under the general title of "Dārṣṭāntika-Sautrāntika," without examining carefully the development of this concept within a span of at least five hundred years. In my own study, I attempt to examine the different layers of the evolution of this concept by analyzing carefully the various arguments proposed by different Dārṣṭāntika-Sautrāntika masters. Chapter 2 and the current chapter on Vasubandhu are examples of such an attempt.

As we know, Vasubandhu, with his numerous writings, is a key figure in the progress or formation of several important Buddhist philosophical schools, including Sarvāstivāda, Dārṣṭāntika-Sautrāntika, and Yogācāra. By examining Vasubandhu's arguments for the cognition of nonexistent objects, we will have a better idea of this central Dārṣṭāntika-Sautrāntika concept and its relationship with the Mahāsāṃghika and Yogācāra concepts. Hopefully, my study can contribute to a somewhat better understanding of the relationship between Dārṣṭāntika, Sautrāntika, and Yogācāra, an issue that has always been interesting, but attracted more attention in recent years.[1]

4.1 Vaibhāṣika Arguments for the Existence of the Past and the Future

Unlike the cases of the Mahāsāṃghikas and early Dārṣṭāntikas, in studying Vasubandhu's concept of the cognition of nonexistent objects, we do not have to rely on scattered sources. Nor do we have to learn his views only through the eyes of his opponents. Vasubandhu left us extensive writings, in which we can find rather systematic arguments for this concept. These arguments were further refuted, equally extensively, by his critic Saṃghabhadra. With these rich sources, we can learn how this concept is conceived in Vasubandhu's own right as well as in the eyes of his opponent. Moreover, we have the advantage of identifying the background and context in which the concept was developed.

A general and less explicit context is the discussion on latent defilements (*anuśaya*). The main section of the text under discussion appears, curiously, in the fifth chapter on latent defilements in AKBh. However, this is not surprising if we recall that the concept of the cognition of nonexistent objects originated in the Mahāsāṃghika discussions on latent defilements and the nonexistence of their objects. The early Dārṣṭāntikas in MV also argued for this concept on the basis of the unreal objects of conjunction (*saṃyoga*). Although the Vaibhāṣikas, the orthodox Sarvāstivādins, refuted their views, the issue is somehow associated with the theme of latent defilements. As a matter of fact, the Vaibhāṣikas do not distinguish between latent defilements (*anuśaya*) and defilements (*kleśa*) in general for they hold that both are bound to their objects. By contrast, the Mahāsāṃghikas hold that *anuśaya*, being a *latent* mental state, has no objects, and it only possesses an object when becoming a manifested defilement (*paryavasthāna*). For the Vaibhāṣikas, a person is bound to objects of the past, present, and future by defilements, either latent or manifested. Then a natural question arises: Do things in the past and future exist?

The question leads to the specific and explicit context that the cognition of nonexistent objects is disputed. If things in the past and future do not exist, then it is impossible to say that a person is bound to these objects by defilements, or that he can be liberated from them. If things in the past and future really exist, then it means that they always exist and are thus eternal. But this goes against the basic Buddhist teaching of impermanence. The Vaibhāṣikas maintain that past and future phenomena really exist, but they are not eternal for they are endowed with the characteristics (*lakṣaṇa*) of conditioned things.

The Vaibhāṣika opponent in AKBh outlines four arguments to support this view. Two of them resort to scriptural authority. In a *sūtra* passage, the Buddha speaks about the existence of the past and future material form (*rūpa*).[2] In another *sūtra* passage, the Buddha speaks more generally about the conditions for the arising of cognition or consciousness: "Consciousness is produced by reason of two. What are these two? The organ of sight and a visible thing . . . the mental organ (*manas*) and *dharmas*."[3] Mental consciousness (*manovijñāna*) is believed to be able to cognize the past and future *dharmas*. Now if they do not exist, mental consciousness would not arise because of the lack of one condition.

This discussion on conditions of cognition leads to the first argument from reasoning: "[The consciousness] has an existent object."[4] The Vaibhāṣika further explains this point: "A consciousness can arise if an object (*viṣaya*) exists (*sati*), but not if it does not exist (*asati*). If past and future things do not exist, there would be consciousness of a nonexistent object (*asadālambanaṃ vijñānaṃ*). Thus in the absence of object (*ālambanābhāvāt*), consciousness itself would not exist."[5] This crucial statement is known as the epistemological argument for the existence of the past and the future. There are many issues involved with this dense argument, such as the exact meaning of existence (*sati*) or nonexistence (*asati*), the difference between consciousness with a nonexistent object and consciousness in the absence of object. We shall treat them in due course in the chapter.

The final Vaibhāṣika argument has to do with the central Buddhist idea of *karma* or action. A good or bad action can give forth a result. At the moment when the result is produced, the retributive cause is past. If the past does not exist, then action cannot produce any result. Note that this argument focuses only on the past. Some Vibhajyavādins, for example, Kāśyapīyas, probably convinced by this argument, concede that the past actions that have not yet given result can also be said to exist.[6]

With these four arguments from scripture and reasoning, the Vaibhāṣika concludes that both the past and the future exist, and only those who affirm the existence of the *dharmas* of all three times are qualified as a *sarvāstivāda* ("a believer in the existence of all").

4.2 Conditions of Cognition

After presenting the Vaibhāṣika arguments, Vasubandhu starts to formulate his own arguments against them. Following Puguang and Fabao, two Chinese commentators of AKBh, La Vallée Poussin attributed Vasubandhu's arguments to the Sautrāntika by interpolating the phrase "the Sautrāntika criticizes."[7] This is based on the understanding that Vasubandhu, in the prose part of AKBh, subscribes to the views of Sautrāntika, especially when he is arguing against the Vaibhāṣika orthodoxy. But the relationship between Vasubandhu and the Sautrāntika is controversial. Some hold that Vasubandhu himself created the label of "Sautrāntika" to designate his real Yogācāra stance, and Vasubandhu was the very first Sautrāntika, but in the sense of a disguised Yogācāra.[8] I would rather hold a more traditional view that takes Sautrāntika as a movement of a great variety of loosely connected groups against the Vaibhāṣika orthodoxy.

This movement had started with the early Dārṣṭāntika masters, and joined forces with Kumāralāta, Harivarman, Śrīlāta, and Vasubandhu. With regard to some key issues, for example, simultaneous causation (*sahabhūhetu*), Vasubandhu holds different views from other Sautrāntika masters such as Śrīlāta (Dhammajoti 2007a: 26; Katō 1989: 218–20). Therefore, I will distinguish Vasubandhu's own views from those of the Sautrāntika he quotes. In Saṃghabhadra's criticism of Vasubandhu, he distinguishes the views of the Dārṣṭāntikas, Kośakāra (the author of AKBh, i.e., Vasubandhu), and the Sthavira (Śrīlāta). Actually, we will see Vasubandhu's arguments on the cognition of nonexistent objects in some respects are quite distinctive from those of early Dārṣṭāntikas and other Sautrāntika masters such as Harivarman and Śrīlāta.

Vasubandhu's first argument aims at the Vaibhāṣika's reference to the *sūtra* passage on conditions of cognition that we cited earlier. According to this passage, consciousness, whether sensory or mental, arises on the basis of two conditions: senses and their respective objects. In the case of mental consciousness, its sense is *manas* or the mental organ, which is not an "organ" in its proper sense. Rather, it is taken to be the previous continuous consciousness that gives rise to the consciousness of the next moment.[9] The object of mental consciousness is *dharma*, or, more precisely, all *dharma*s. Since what is under dispute is exactly what *dharma* means or comprises, for now we understand *dharma* simply as that which is knowable of mental consciousness, which virtually covers everything.

With regard to the two conditions, Vasubandhu insists that they play different roles: the mental organ is a generating condition (*janaka-pratyaya*), whereas *dharma*s are conditions in a quality of object (*ālambana-pratyaya*). So when mental consciousness arises, he asks, "Are these *dharma*s, similar to the mental organ, acting as its generating condition, or are they only [conditions] in a quality of object (*ālambanamātra*)?"[10] Apparently, he is in favor of the latter option.

Vasubandhu uses the example of future *dharma*s to support his view. Evidently, future *dharma*s, which will exist after thousands of years or which will never exist, cannot be the generating condition of a present mental consciousness. To understand this example, we need to clarify two basic features of the generating condition. First, as his commentator Yaśomitra puts it, "the posterior cause of a previous effect is unreasonable."[11] In other words, a generating cause or condition cannot be temporally posterior to its effect. Now if future *dharma*s act as the generating condition of the present mental consciousness, then it would mean that the cause is temporarily posterior to its effect, which is taken to be unreasonable by Vasubandhu and Yaśomitra. Whether Vasubandhu here also rejects simultaneous causation is unclear, but elsewhere in AKBh, he does endorse this type of causation.

The second feature of generating condition is made explicit by Saṃghabhadra, Vasubandhu's critic, who says: "If you (=Vasubandhu) say that the mental organ and the consciousness that arises on the basis of it are of the same continuum without intervals, and that [the former] that gives rise to [the latter] can be called a generating [condition], but *dharma*s cannot be thus called, then . . ."[12] In other words, if *x* gives rise to *y*, then *x* and *y* must be of the same continuum without intervals. *Dharma*s, by definition, are not of the same mental continuum as mental consciousness and the mental organ. Hence, *dharma*s cannot be the generating condition of mental consciousness. If there is an interval of thousands of years between *dharma*s and mental consciousness, it would be even more impossible for *dharma*s to play this role.

At this juncture, Saṃghabhadra criticizes Vasubandhu for being inconsistent. For instance, if we apply Vasubandhu's analysis to the case of visual consciousness arising on the basis of eyes and material form, then the visual organ (i.e., eyes) should be the generating condition of visual consciousness, but they are not of the same continuum at all, one being material, the other mental.[13] Moreover, Vasubandhu denies that *dharma*s of the far future ("after thousands of years") can be the generating condition of the present mental consciousness, but how about *dharma*s of the near future? For Saṃghabhadra, *dharma*s of the far or near future are of the same nature, serving as the objective condition of mental consciousness. "The mental organ, being the basis (*āśraya*) of mental consciousness, acts as the generating condition; *dharma*s, being the object [of mental consciousness], give rise to mental consciousness. Although a basis is different from an object, they share the same meaning of generating condition."[14]

Vasubandhu uses *nirvāṇa* as a further example to argue for the view that *dharma*s can only be objects of cognition, but not its generating condition. *Nirvāṇa*, being an unconditioned *dharma*, is defined as "the cessation of all arising."[15] Since it is contradictory to all arising, *nirvāṇa* cannot give rise to mental consciousness, and cannot be its generating condition. As Yaśomitra comments: "*Nirvāṇa*, because of its cessation, cannot give rise to [mental] consciousness."[16]

With the support of both cases of future *dharma*s and *nirvāṇa*, Vasubandhu concludes that *dharma*s can be merely the object of cognition without acting as its generating condition. On the contrary, Saṃghabhadra, taking a Vaibhāṣika point of view, insists that both the object and the basis of consciousness are the generating condition of a consciousness, hence it is necessary for a consciousness to arise with two conditions: its basis and object.

There are some other proposals to bypass this Vaibhāṣika dogma of two conditions of cognition. Harivarman proposes that "only for the purpose of rejecting the view of self (*ātman*), it is thus said that all consciousnesses arise on the basis of two conditions, but not four."[17] The Vaiśeṣikas, an orthodox Hindu philosophical school, believe that a combination of self, mind (*manas*), sense (*indriya*), and object produces a consciousness. The Buddha rejects the roles of self and mind, and hence speaks of two conditions instead of four. This teaching of the Buddha can only be seen as a conventional, but not necessary truth.[18] Kamalaśīla, a Yogācāra-Mādhyamika, holds that "there are two types of consciousness: one with objects and the other without objects (*anālambana*). With regard to consciousness with objects, the World-honored One speaks of 'consciousness arising on the basis of two conditions.'"[19]

Kamalaśīla's opinion makes sense in limiting the scope of this teaching of the Buddha to cognition with objects. However, the cases where this teaching does not apply include not only cognition without objects (*anālambana*), but also cognition with nonexistent objects (*asadālambana*), which is exactly what Vasubandhu is arguing for. For him, a crucial step to establish the cognition with nonexistent objects is that objects of cognition do not have to act as the generating condition of cognition, that is, the condition that gives rise to cognition, but are merely its objective condition, that is, the condition in a quality of object. Then, nonexistents such as the past and the future would possibly become objects of cognition. Vasubandhu thus concludes his first argument: "If *dharmas* can be merely objects of cognition (*ālambanamātra*), then I claim that the past and the future are also objects of cognition,"[20] which leads to his next argument.

4.3 Speaking of the Past and the Future

As compared to the earlier argument from the past and the future developed among the Mahāsāṃghika subgroups and early Yogācāras, Vasubandhu's argument is more elaborate and sophisticated. As Saṃghabhadra's detailed refutation of his argument is also preserved, we are going to examine their debate on the existence of the past and the future in three aspects: linguistically speaking of the past and the future, epistemologically knowing them, and their ontological status.

In speaking of the past and the future, we encounter some puzzling features of the existential verb in Sanskrit. For instance, the Buddha did speak of "*asty atītam asty anāgatam*" (AKBh 299,6–7), literally meaning "the past exists (*asti*) and the future exists (*asti*)." But according to Vasubandhu, here "the word '*asti*' is irregular."[21] Alternatively, we can translate the Buddha's saying as "There *is* the past and there *is* the future." The subtle difference between the two English expressions becomes more significant in understanding the following Sanskrit sentence: "*asti dīpasya prāgabhāvo 'sti paścādabhāva iti*" (AKBh 299,7–8). If we translate *asti* into "to exist," it runs like this: "The previous nonexistence of the lamp exists; the posterior nonexistence of the lamp exists." We have a self-contradictory statement: the lamp is nonexistent, and yet it exists. Alternatively, we can translate the sentence as follows: "There *is* (*asti*) previous nonexistence of the lamp; there *is* (*asti*) posterior nonexistence of the lamp." This way the tension between nonexistence and existence is eased as the phrase "there is" is broader than the term "to exist." Vasubandhu provides us with another example: "*asti niruddhaḥ sa dīpo na tu mayā nirodhita iti*" (AKBh 299,8–9). This sentence is unintelligible if we translate *asti* as "to exist": "The lamp exists extinction, but it [was] not extinguished by me." There is an apparent contradiction between the lamp's existence and extinction. The word *asti* here should be understood as a copula rather than an existential verb; hence the sentence means: "The lamp *is* (*asti*) extinguished, but it [was] not extinguished by me."

The source of the problem goes back to the overlapping or confusion between copula and existential verb in almost all Indo-European languages. In contrast, the two types of words are clearly distinguished in some non-Indo-European languages such as Chinese and Arabic (Graham 1965). English, though an Indo-European language, has a tendency to distinguish "to be" from "to exist," and hence its copula and existential verb are less easily confused. That is why we can make better sense of these sentences in their English translation than in their Sanskrit original.

Without the convenience of distinguishing the copula from the existential verb in Sanskrit, Vasubandhu came up with an alternative solution to the problem. He says:

> We also say that there is (*asti*) the past and there is (*asti*) the future.[22] The past is that which existed previously (*bhūtapūrva*). The future is that which, given its cause exists (*sati*), will exist (*bhaviṣyati*). It is in this sense that we say that there is (*asti*) [the past, as well as the future].[23] But they are not substantial entities (*dravyatas*).[24]

Substantial entities refer to existents in the present. For Vasubandhu, neither the past nor the future can exist as does the present, rather they only existed previously or will exist. In other words, he would admit that there *are* the past and the future, but they *do not exist* now. In this sense, the term "to be" (*asti*) not only has its normal meaning of "to exist," but also can mean "not to exist." Xuanzang's Chinese translation states explicitly: "The word 'is' (*asti*) is applied to what exists, as well as to what does not exist."[25]

To argue against this interpretation, Vasubandhu's Vaibhāṣika interlocutor refers to another *sūtra* passage: "Past action (*karma*) which has been destroyed, which has perished, and which has ceased, does exist (*asti*)."[26] This passage has more to do with the Vaibhāṣika argument from *karma* for the existence of the past and the future. Given the general Buddhist soteriological framework, it seems difficult to hold that past action merely existed previously. For it implies the denial of the karmic causation.

Vasubandhu responds that when the Buddha said that past action exists, he had in view its power of giving forth a result, a power that was placed in the series of the agent through action which has now passed away. "To understand otherwise, that is, if [past action exists] at the present in and of itself (*svena bhāvena*), it cannot be considered as past."[27] To support his position, Vasubandhu quotes from the *Paramārthaśūnyatāsūtra*: "The eye, arising, does not come from any place; perishing, it does not remain in any place. In this way, Oh Bhikṣus, the eye exists (*bhavati*) after having been nonexistent (*abhūtvā*), after having existed (*bhūtvā*), disappears."[28] Though a short passage, it provides Vasubandhu with enough scriptural authority to challenge the Vaibhāṣika view on the existence of the past and the future.[29]

As we will discuss more in this chapter, if the past and the future exist, it would be difficult to account for becoming and change. The foundational Buddhist teaching of impermanence (*anitya*) is, however, committed to becoming and change, and requires one to account for it. In this *sūtra*, the eye is arising and disappearing by going through a sequence of nonexistence–existence–nonexistence, which corresponds respectively to its future, present, and past states. If a future eye existed, the Buddha would not have said that the eye exists only after having been nonexistent (*abhūtvā bhavati*).

So far it seems that Vasubandhu has made a convincing case for the nonexistence of the past and the future. According to him, "there is (*asti*) the past and there is (*asti*) the future," but it does not necessarily mean that "the past and the future exist (*asti*)." In a linguistic tradition where copula and existential verb are to a great extent confused, Vasubandhu has made a significant contribution in distinguishing "to be" from "to exist," and hence we can meaningfully speak of the past and the future without being committed to their existence.

4.4 Cognition of the Past and the Future

If the past and the future are nonexistent, then can we know them? And how can we know them? To be known, they have to be objects of cognition. However, "if they do not exist, how can they be objects of cognition (*ālambana*)?"[30] Vasubandhu says: "They are (*asti*) in the manner in which they are taken as objects of cognition."[31] The past is taken as object with the mark of the past, that is, having existed (*abhūt*), while the future with the mark of the future, that is, coming into existence (*bhaviṣyati*).

Vasubandhu asks us to reflect our experiences of memory and anticipation. While recollecting a certain thing or feeling of the past, we do not perceive it as vividly as it exists (*asti*) at the present. Instead, we remember the way it has existed (*abhūt*). Similarly, we can only anticipate a future thing or sensation in the way it will exist (*bhaviṣyati*), but not in the way that it exists at the present.

Saṃghabhadra, however, thinks that Vasubandhu misses an important point in his phenomenological descriptions. That is, any experience of memory or anticipation has to be based on perception at the present. Without such a basis, it is impossible to distinguish these experiences from purely illusory cognitions such as perceiving a person in place of a pillar, or a dove in place of a piece of wood. An object that has existed or will exist has its basis in the object that exists now. Otherwise, these past or future objects would become pure illusion.[32]

Vasubandhu seems to have anticipated this objection. He agrees that the present object is involved in the experiences of memory and anticipation. Only if we experience a thing at the present can we then recall this object at a later time. "The way that a past [object] is remembered is like the way a present material form is experienced."[33] When anticipating a certain object in the future, we also imagine that it will be like the present object, being grasped by a cognition. "If this [object of memory or anticipation] exists (*asti*) just like [the present object], then a present [object] is attained. If it does not exist (*nāsti*), [but has existed or will exist], then it is established that there is [the cognition] of nonexistent objects."[34] In other words, perception of a present object is the cognition of existent objects, whereas memory or anticipation of a past or future object is the cognition of nonexistent objects.

For Saṃghabhadra, however, Vasubandhu is contradicting himself. If he said that we do not perceive a past object as vividly as it exists at the present, but only remember the way it has existed, then he should not say that the way that a past object is remembered is like the way that a present object is experienced. It is evident that when we perceive an existing object, we are *not* recollecting a past object. Similarly, when we remember an object that has existed, we do *not* perceive a present object. Perception and memory, existing and having existed, should be sharply distinguished.[35]

I think Vasubandhu would admit to such a distinction too. The reason for him to mention the similarities between memory, anticipation, and perception is to distance them from illusory experiences. A variety of illusions are used by the Dārṣṭāntikas as supportive cases for the cognition of nonexistent objects.[36] In his arguments for the same concept, Vasubandhu seems never to refer to a single case of illusion. However, when he treats objects of memory and anticipation as nonexistent objects, the same status as illusory objects, their distinction from illusions is blurred. For Saṃghabhadra, at least in the case of memory, it would make more sense to admit the existence of its objects. He says:

> If one remembers a past [object] like the way of [perceiving] a present existent, and holds that the past object is (*asti*, alternatively, exists) in the manner in which it is taken as object of cognition (*ālambana*), then it is established that the past really exists. Because we remember the past [object] as existence in the manner of experiencing a real existent at the present. If you admit its existence as recollected, how is it possible that the past is not really existent?[37]

Although Saṃghabhadra's Vaibhāṣika view makes a bit more sense in the case of the past object, and hence convinced some Vibhajyavādins, it is more difficult to argue for the existence of the future object. Vasubandhu brings up this issue with the example of sound. The issue at stake is: "What is the object of [the cognition] which takes as object the previous nonexistence of sound?"[38] This question itself can be credited to the Dārṣṭāntikas,[39] but Vasubandhu elaborates it in further details.

Vasubandhu's Vaibhāṣika interlocutor answers that the object of this cognition is "the sound itself" (*śabda eva*). Vasubandhu thinks this is unreasonable, since it would mean that "anyone who is in quest of the [previous] nonexistence of sound should make a noise."[40] The Vaibhāṣika further clarifies that he means "the future state" (*anāgatāvastha*) of the sound itself. But it still does not make sense, because, according to the Vaibhāṣika theory, the future state of sound is existent (*sati*), how can it be understood as nonexistent (*nāsti*), that is, the previous nonexistence (*prāgabhāva*) of sound? If the Vaibhāṣika holds that "nonexistence" here means that "it does not presently exist" (*vartamāno nāsti*), Vasubandhu thinks that the Vaibhāṣika cannot legitimately speak of the difference between the future and the present in this manner because he takes the past, present, and future as of the same nature (*ekatvāt*). If, however, he would like to acknowledge the difference between the future and present sounds in terms of nonexistence versus existence, then it establishes Vasubandhu's own theory of "existence after not having existed" (*abhūtvābhāva*).

In this debate, Vasubandhu is attacking a weak point of the Vaibhāṣikas. On the one hand, they hold that all the three times exist; on the other hand, they try to account for various types of nonexistence (*abhāva*) as developed among Indian philosophers, Buddhist and non-Buddhist. Hence they would have to endorse a self-contradictory statement: A future—therefore *existent*—sound is the previous *nonexistence* of sound. To resolve this self-contradiction, Vasubandhu would hold that the previous nonexistence of sound is the future *nonexistent* sound. Therefore, the short answer to the question under discussion is: "The object of the cognition which takes as object the previous nonexistence of sound is *nonexistence*." This way, Vasubandhu has proved that "both existence (*bhāva*) and nonexistence (*abhāva*) can be an object of consciousness."[41]

In defense of the Vaibhāṣika position, Saṃgabhadra provides an interesting account of the issue. He revises the Vaibhāṣika view by making the following proposal:

> Regarding the consciousness that takes as object the previous nonexistence of sound, its object is not the sound itself, but the supporting condition (*adhiṣṭhāna*) where the sound will be. This means that its object is only the

> various things on which the sound will be located. Since they are in a state that the sound has not yet occurred, they are taken to be the nonexistence of sound.[42]

In this proposal, Saṃghabhadra insists on the Vaibhāṣika view that the object of cognition has to be something existent, rather than nonexistent. If the sound itself fails the test, then try the supporting condition of sound. In the location where the sound will be, there surely exist various things, so the supporting condition is existent. Meanwhile, since the sound has not yet occurred in this location, it is the *nonexistence* of sound. The earlier contradiction between existence and nonexistence is thus resolved.

A key point in his resolution is to reduce previous nonexistence (*prāgabhāva*) to mutual nonexistence (*anyonyābhāva*). Together with posterior nonexistence (*dhvaṃsa*) and absolute nonexistence (*atyantābhāva*), they are the four types of nonexistence generally accepted among major schools of Indian philosophy, including Buddhism. But there were attempts to reduce all the four types to mutual nonexistence, which can then be analyzed into the mutual exclusion of two beings, as Saṃghabhadra points out: "All the mutual nonexistents must be taken as being based upon existents."[43] This way he has successfully defended the existent status of the future sound, and reduced the cognition of the previous nonexistence of sound to a cognition of existent objects, that is, the supporting condition where the sound will be. As I will show in Chapter 7, the same strategy in dealing with negative judgments is found in the later Buddhist philosopher Dharmakīrti and contemporary philosopher Edmund Husserl.

4.5 Ontological Status of the Past and the Future

In their debates on the linguistic and epistemological issues, both Vasubandhu and his Vaibhāṣika opponent have indicated their respective ontological commitments. Now let us examine in more detail their different views on the ontological status of the past and the future. One example is illustrative. Saṃghabhadra is questioned by an interlocutor without clear school affiliation: "Whether the future lamp has lighted or not?" Then a dilemma is formulated: if it has lighted, then no difference is found between the present and future lamps; "if it does not light, then it cannot in itself be a lamp."[44] In facing this dilemma, Saṃghabhadra explains that "the past and the future in themselves (*svabhāva*, *ti* 體) exist, but their function (*kāritra*, *yong* 用) does not exist."[45] This means that the past and future lamps have no function of lighting, but they themselves exist. Why? "The past and the future themselves (*svabhāva*) are taken to be existent because they, being *dharma*s to be known, have the nature of knowable (*jñeyatva*)."[46] Saṃghabhadra seems to have adopted a Vaiśeṣika view that takes the knowable to be identical to existence. This is also his rationale for developing an epistemological argument for the existence of the past and the future:

> Whatever is knowable is existent.
> The past and the future are knowable.
> Therefore, the past and the future exist.

Examining this argument more carefully, however, one will find that it is more or less a circular argument: an epistemological argument is based on an epistemological definition of existence itself, which never touches its ontological grounds.

Vasubandhu's Vaibhāṣika interlocutor takes a different approach by holding that past and future objects are nothing but atoms in a state of dispersion (*vikīrṇa*). In contrast, present objects are atoms in a state of combination (*saṃcaya*). Objects across all the three times exist; their difference lies only in their atoms being in a state of dispersion or combination.

Vasubandhu comes up with several reasons to refute this Vaibhāṣika claim. First, both parties agree that past and future objects are knowable, but for

Vasubandhu, "they are never grasped in the form of dispersion."[47] Hence, the claim is not vindicated epistemologically. Second, if all the material things are explained in terms of the dispersion or combination of atoms, then the atoms would become eternal. "There would be no any [atom] arising or ceasing."[48] This way, it would fail to account for any change, violate the foundational Buddhist teaching of impermanence, and fall into the heresy of Ājīvikas, one of the major rivals of early Buddhism. If we follow the view as found in the *Paramārthaśūnyatāsūtra* instead, impermanence and change can be explained as "existence after having been nonexistence and disappearance after having existed" (*abhūtvā bhavati bhūtvā ca prativigacchati*) (cited earlier). Third, mental factors such as feeling (*vedanā*) are not made of atoms. How can they be interpreted as the dispersion or combination of atoms?

Having refuted the Vaibhāṣika theory on the ontological status of the past and the future, Vasubandhu concludes this argument with a further proof of the cognition of nonexistent objects. With regard to the feeling that is just mentioned, if we remember a past feeling as it was experienced when it was present, then this feeling would be, like atoms, eternal, which is not admissible. Alternatively, "if [the past feeling that is remembered] is not like [the feeling that is experienced at the present], then it is proved that there is [the cognition] of nonexistent objects."[49]

4.6 Absolute Nonexistence

Having discussed the past and the future, which correspond respectively to posterior nonexistence and previous nonexistence, Vasubandhu moves on to a third type of nonexistence, that is, absolute nonexistence (*atyantābhāva*). Taken to be the most extreme type of nonexistence, in an Indian context it is usually exemplified by the hair of a turtle, the horn of a hare, or the son of a barren woman. Vasubandhu here uses the example of the thirteenth sense-sphere (*āyatana*).

A popular way to characterize reality among Buddhist philosophers is to classify it into twelve sense-spheres, which comprise six senses (eye, ear, nose, tongue, body, and mental organ) and their respective objects (visible form, sound, smell, taste, the tangible, and *dharma*). The category of twelve sense-spheres is believed to cover all that is existent, so there is not a thirteenth sense-sphere. Exactly for this reason, the thirteenth sense-sphere becomes an example of absolute nonexistence.

Vasubandhu's Vaibhāṣika interlocutor challenges his concept of the cognition of nonexistent objects with this example of absolute nonexistence: "If nonexistence (*asad*) can be the object of cognition, then a thirteenth sense-sphere also could be [the object of cognition]."[50] For the Vaibhāṣika, "nonexistence," in its proper sense, means absolute nonexistence such as the thirteenth sense-sphere. A nonexistent object of cognition is impossible. If it is an object of cognition, then it is existent. If, however, it is nonexistent, then it cannot be an object of cognition. And in this case, the cognition can be considered as having no object rather than having a nonexistent object. At this juncture, Saṃghabhadra fiercely criticizes Vasubandhu for upholding a self-contradictory position:

> It is self-contradictory for him (=Vasubandhu) to say that there is the cognition (*buddhi*) of nonexistent objects. If cognition has objects, then he should not say that these objects are nonexistent; if objects are nonexistent, then he should not say that this cognition has objects. Since nonexistence means nothing altogether. If what he means is that the objects of this cognition themselves are nothing altogether, he should explicitly say that this cognition has no objects. Why does he act like a coward and deceive us by saying that there is cognition that takes nonexistents as objects? Therefore, there is definitely no cognition that takes nonexistents as objects.[51]

Vasubandhu's response is rather clever. He asks his interlocutor: "Then what is the object of a consciousness (*vijñāna*) which consists in saying, 'A thirteenth sense-sphere does not exist (*nāsti*).' "[52] By saying "a thirteenth sense-sphere does not exist," it is presupposed that we *know* that a thirteenth sense-sphere does not exist. This cognition or consciousness must have an object, then what is it?

The Vaibhāṣika answers: "The object of this [consciousness] is just its name ['thirteenth sense-sphere']."[53] According to the Vaibhāṣika theory, name (*nāman*) is classified as one of the conditionings dissociated from mind (*cit taviprayuktasaṃskāra*), which is existent. So the cognition that takes this name as object is a cognition of existent rather than nonexistent objects. As a matter of fact, one scheme of classifying different modes of existence among the Vaibhāṣikas lists nominal existence (**nāmasat*) as one of the five types of existence, and the examples singled out include the hair of a turtle, the horn of a hare, and sky-flower.[54] This way, the Vaibhāṣikas have expelled nonexistence from our scope of knowledge, as the ancient Greek philosopher Parmenides had proposed. Whatever we talk about or think of is at least a nominal existence, and we can never countenance nonexistence.

For Vasubandhu, however, if the object of this cognition is the name "thirteenth sense-sphere," then the earlier proposition can be reformulated as "the name 'thirteenth sense-sphere' does not exist." But this is contradictory to the Vaibhāṣika's own theory that names are existent. Since the Vaibhāṣika's position is self-defeating, Vasubandhu establishes the concept of the cognition of nonexistent objects once again in the case of absolute nonexistence.

4.7 Doubts

Vasubandhu's final argument has to do with doubts (*vimarśa*). His Vaibhāṣika opponent quotes a *sūtra* passage for support: "It is an impossible state that I know, that I see that which does not exist (*nāsti*) in this world."[55] The same passage is quoted by Harivarman's opponent in JP and by Īśvara in the

Abhidharmadīpa to support the Vaibhāṣika position.[56] Its exact parallel is not found in Chinese Āgamas or Pāli Nikāyas, but a similar passage is included in the *Madhyama Āgama*, where the Buddha shared his experience of seeing light during meditation with his disciples. He had doubts with regard to this light: "If there is no such [light] in the world, can I see or know it?"[57] Because of the doubt, he lost concentration in meditation and his vision of light also disappeared.

In Vasubandhu's understanding, this passage does not support the Vaibhāṣika view that negates the cognition of nonexistent objects. Instead, the Buddha is meant to say: "I am not like other prideful (*ābhimānika*) ascetics who perceive a nonexistent light (*avabhāsa*) as existent. As for me, I only perceive as existing that which exists (*asti*)."[58] In other words, the Buddha did not deny the possibility for the ascetics to cognize a nonexistent light, but only disapproved their claim that the light exists.

Moreover, if the Vaibhāṣika thesis that "all cognitions have existent objects (*sadālambana*)"[59] is correct, then there is no longer any place for doubts (*vimarśa*). For Vasubandhu, doubts are possible only if one has to decide between existent and nonexistent objects. If all objects of cognition were existent, then all their cognitions would be assertive and true. But this is counterintuitive.

Saṃghabhadra disagrees with Vasubandhu's interpretation. First of all, a nonexistent light cannot appear as existent for the ascetics to perceive. If the nonexistent light can be perceived, then a thirteenth sense-sphere can also be perceived. As we discussed earlier, the thirteenth sense-sphere is absolute nonexistent. So the *sūtra* passage is meant to say that other prideful ascetics claim to perceive the light that has *not yet* appeared, but the Buddha only perceives the existent light as light. It indicates a difference between the wrong knowledge of ascetics and the right knowledge of the Buddha. For Saṃghabhadra, "because all cognitions have existent objects, one can have doubts about these objects, wondering whether he has right or wrong knowledge about the perceived objects."[60] The difference between right and wrong can only be found within existent objects, and doubts arise in the face of the uncertainty between right and wrong. Nonexistence, unlike existence, cannot be differentiated; hence no difference of right or wrong, good or bad can be found within nonexistence itself, or between nonexistence and existence. Therefore, he thinks his Vaibhāṣika account of doubts is more reasonable.

Vasubandhu quotes another *sūtra* passage to support his own position:

> Now, Bhikṣus! My disciple, being instructed by me in the morning, makes progress by the evening, being instructed in the evening, makes progress by the morning. He will know that which exists as existence and that which does not exist as nonexistence (*sac ca satto jñāsyaty asac cāsattaḥ*), that which is not the highest as not the highest, that which is the highest (*anuttara*) as the highest.[61]

The same passage is quoted in YBh to support the Yogācāra arguments for the cognition of nonexistent objects.[62] This passage indicates that the Buddha would possibly agree with Vasubandhu's concept of the cognition of nonexistent objects as he explicitly mentioned the knowledge of that which does not exist as nonexistence. Hence, Vasubandhu concludes that the Vaibhāṣika argument for the existence of the past and the future is an unsound argument (*ahetu*) since it relies on an unestablished premise: "All cognitions have existent objects."

Still, Saṃghabhadra has another way of defending the Vaibhāṣika position. He argues that the word "*sat*" in this passage does not mean "existence," rather it means "good." Accordingly, *asat* means "bad" rather than "nonexistence."[63] So the passage has nothing to do with the cognition of existent or nonexistent objects; rather, it is meant to encourage the disciple to strive for the good and the highest, that is, *nirvāṇa*.

4.8 Six Arguments

I have examined Vasubandhu's theory of the cognition of nonexistent objects by organizing them into six main arguments. All of them are aimed to refute the Vaibhāṣika view that the past and the future exist. In particular, the Vaibhāṣikas developed an epistemological argument for their view:

1. Whatever is knowable is existent.
2. The past and the future are knowable.
3. Therefore, the past and the future exist.

To substantiate premise 1, the Vaibhāṣikas hold that a cognition is possible with two conditions, a basis (i.e., sense) and an object (i.e., the knowable), and both act as generating conditions (*janaka-pratyaya*). Since a nonexistent cannot produce anything, it cannot be a generating condition of cognition and hence is not an object of cognition. Therefore, whatever is knowable or an object of cognition, it must be existent.

Vasubandhu's Argument One focuses on the conditions of cognition. He agrees that both conditions are necessary, but they function differently: the sense is a generating condition, while the knowable is a condition in a quality of object (*ālambana-pratyaya*). He uses the examples of future *dharma*s and *nirvāṇa* to illustrate this point. Both are no doubt knowable, but they cannot give rise to any cognition. Because a cause, that is, future *dharmas*, cannot be temporally posterior to its effect, that is, their cognition at the present. Whereas *nirvāṇa* is, by definition, the cessation of all arising. If these objects do not have to act as the generating condition of their cognition, but are merely its objective condition, then nonexistents, though lacking any generating power, can still be objects of cognition. Therefore, it is established that there is the cognition of nonexistent objects and premise 1 is falsified.

With regard to premise 2, the two parties are not disputing on *whether* the past and the future are knowable, but they disagree on *how* they are known, that is, whether they are known as existents or nonexistents. In Argument Two, Vasubandhu starts with linguistic issues. In Sanskrit, when one says "*asty atītam asty anāgatam*," it can mean "there is (*asti*) the past and there is (*asti*) the future," or "the past exists (*asti*) and the future exists (*asti*)." This is because copula and existential verb are to a great extent confused in Sanskrit and other Indo-European languages. Vasubandhu thinks that the word *asti* is applied to what exists, as well as to what does not exist. The past does not exist, but it "existed previously"; the future does not exist, but it "will exist." Therefore, we can say "there are the past and the future," but it does not necessarily mean that "the past and the future exist."

In Argument Three, Vasubandhu addresses the question: "If the past and the future do not exist, how can they be objects of cognition?" The short answer is that the past is taken as object with the mark of the past, that is, having existed, while the future with the mark of the future, that is, coming into existence. He further illustrates this view with the experience of memory and the cognition of the previous nonexistence of sound. In both cases, these past and future objects have to be nonexistents rather than existents. Argument Four is concerned with the ontological status of the past and the future, and Vasubandhu does not agree with the Vaibhāṣika view that past and future objects are nothing other than atoms in a state of dispersion. He thinks that this would make atoms eternal entities and violate the foundational Buddhist teaching of impermanence.

All the arguments in this chapter have proved that the past and the future, that is, posterior nonexistence and previous nonexistence, can be objects of cognition. In Argument Five, Vasubandhu moves on to the most extreme type of nonexistence—absolute nonexistence—and discusses the cognition which consists in saying, "A thirteenth sense-sphere does not exist." Here "a thirteenth sense-sphere" is an example of absolute nonexistence. The Vaibhāṣikas hold that even in this case the cognition is taking as object the name "thirteenth sense-sphere," which is a nominal existent. But Vasubandhu thinks that the

Vaibhāṣika position is self-defeating, since the earlier proposition can be reformulated as "the name 'thirteenth sense-sphere' does not exist," which would mean that an existent is nonexistent. The final argument from doubts is concerned more with premise 1 again. If the Vaibhāṣika thesis "all cognitions have existent objects" is correct, then there is no longer any place for doubts. Doubts are possible only if one has to decide between existent and nonexistent objects.

Vasubandhu's arguments for the cognition of nonexistent objects mark the final stage of the development of this concept before it was taken over by Buddhist logicians in a new direction and with different terminologies. We can find traces of influence by early schools in many of his arguments. In particular, three of his arguments focus on the cognition of the past and the future. As I have discussed in Chapter 1, this type of argument most probably originated in the Mahāsāṃghika subgroup Uttarāpathaka and was accepted and further developed among the Vibhajyavādins, including the Mahīśāsakas and the Dharmaguptakas. Early Yogācāras also took it as one of their main arguments. As I have acknowledged earlier, the specific argument from the cognition of the previous nonexistence of sound is credited to the Dārṣṭāntikas. The argument from absolute nonexistence can also be traced back to the Dārṣṭāntikas and, less explicitly, to early Yogācāras. And the argument from doubts is similar to the Dārṣṭāntika argument from cognitive error (see Chapter 2; and Cox 1988: 49–51) and the Yogācāra argument from heretical views (see Chapter 3). As compared to his predecessors, Vasubandhu is innovative in his argument from conditions of cognition, especially his distinction between the generating condition and the condition in a quality of object. If we take this concept of the cognition of nonexistent objects as a testing case for Vasubandhu's relationship to various Buddhist philosophical schools, then I would not quickly conclude that Vasubandhu or the Sautrāntika in AKBh is a disguised Yogācāra, because, as we see, he had received influences from almost all directions. So I would rather think that Vasubandhu is a great syncretic.

In this chapter, I mainly study the argument *for* the cognition of nonexistent objects, and cannot deal with the counterarguments of the Vaibhāṣikas and Saṃghabhadra in details. Actually, they deserve much credit for bravely launching onto an intellectual path that leads to the view that everything exists, thus becoming the common enemy for many Buddhist and non-Buddhist philosophical schools. Although holding a more or less unusual view, they find a companion in the ancient Greek philosopher Parmenides. And, according to Priest (2009), Parmenideanism is the orthodox view among contemporary philosophers in the twentieth century. So I would not pretend to show that Vasubandhu had defeated his Vaibhāṣika opponents, rather it is still an open issue regarding whether everything exists or some things exist and some do not. The cognition of nonexistent objects seems to hold a key to resolving this controversial issue.

PART TWO

EPISTEMOLOGICAL APPROACHES TO NONEXISTENCE

5

Non-cognition

In the history of Indian philosophy, we can identify three major figures who contributed to the theory of non-cognition. These are the Mīmāṃsaka Kumārila, the Buddhist Īśvarasena, and the latter's student Dharmakīrti. Whereas we have a large amount of material that attests the thought of Kumārila and Dharmakīrti, sources that allow us to determine Īśvarasena's ideas are very limited in number and are only indirect, as none of his works has survived.

The present chapter will discuss some concepts and material that may be linked to Īśvarasena's ideas. These include the concept of *feiliang* (非量), as found in the writings of Dharmapāla, Asvabhāva, Jinaputra, and their Chinese counterparts, and *apramāṇatā* (or *apramāṇatva*), as found in the works of Dharmakīrti and his commentators. I shall demonstrate that the two concepts in many ways mirror the theory of three *pramāṇa*s, proposed by Īśvarasena.

As most of this data is from the sixth to the eighth century, they are extremely helpful in clarifying the early development of the theory of non-cognition and the interactions between the three aforementioned figures. This is especially true when they are compared with post-Dharmakīrtian Indian commentaries and later Tibetan sources, which constitute the main focus of research for many scholars. In this chapter, the author hopes to fill gaps in our understanding of the early development of this theory, and to respond to Steinkellner's (1992) call for such a study.

5.1 A Third *Pramāṇa*

Kellner (2003: 121) identified three major thinkers who advanced the theory of non-cognition in the history of Indian philosophy. All of them, curiously, were active around the seventh century. The first is Kumārila, a Mīmāṃsaka who left us the voluminous *Ślokavārttika*, which contains a chapter on absence (*abhāva*)—presumably the earliest systematic treatment of such a concept in the history of Indian philosophy.[1] This chapter in turn was criticized by the Buddhist scholar Śāntarakṣita in the eighth century. Kellner (1997a) and Taber (2001) have conducted careful studies of the relevant passages in Kumārila's *Ślokavārttika* and *Tantravārttika*, as well as of some fragments of his lost *Bṛhaṭṭīkā*, which appear to have been preserved in Śāntarakṣita's *Tattvasaṃgraha*. Kumārila, a non-Buddhist and vocal critic of Dignāga, was obviously not bound to the latter's endorsement of only two means of knowledge (*pramāṇa*), that is, perception (*pratyakṣa*) and inference (*anumāna*). In contrast, he proposed six means of knowledge, namely, perception, inference, verbal testimony (*śabda*), analogy (*upamāna*), presumption (*arthāpatti*), and absence (*abhāva*).[2]

The second figure is the Buddhist philosopher Dharmakīrti, who developed the concept of *anupalabdhi* in his various works, and left us with the most sophisticated account of non-cognition in the history of Buddhism. Dharmakīrti strictly follows Dignāga in admitting no more than two means of knowledge. In contrast to the Nyaiyāyikas, who hold that absence is known through perception, he insists that it is known through inference. In Dharmakīrti's view, the fact that "there is *no* pottery on the table" is known through an inferential judgment that is based on the perception of an empty table instead of a table with pottery. He further understands non-cognition (*anupalabdhi*) as one of the three evidences (*hetu*) that ensure sound inferences, and classifies it into various types, in his *Nyāyabindu* up to eleven.[3]

Some scholars, most notably Kellner (1997a,b, 1999, 2001, 2003), have conducted detailed studies of this concept in the works of Dharmakīrti and post-Dharmakīrti commentators. It appears that Dharmakīrti did not develop his theory of non-cognition from scratch. Most probably, he was responding to the third figure, that is, his teacher Īśvarasena, who, in contrast to the other two figures, unfortunately left us no writings, although fragments of his ideas can be found in Dharmakīrti's works. According to Steinkellner (1966) and Katsura (1992), one salient feature of Īśvarasena's view on non-cognition is that he takes it as a separate *pramāṇa* over and above perception and inference, which is exactly the view that Dharmakīrti went to great lengths to refute. Because of Dharmakīrti's great efforts and subsequent influence, we do not see any evidence that Īśvarasena's somewhat "heretic" view was held by post-Dharmakīrti Indian Buddhist philosophers. Therefore, we know very little about this third *pramāṇa* except that it is referred to as the mere absence of cognition (*uplabdhyabhāvamātra*) or mere non-perception (*adarśanamātra*).

Katsura (1992) and Yaita (1984, 1985b) identified some sections of Dignāga's works that mark an early development of this theory. According to Katsura (1992), the fact that Dignāga knew about the idea of non-cognition is indicated in two passages, in chapter five of the *Pramāṇasamuccayavṛtti* and in the *Nyāyamukha* respectively. The first passage is in a context of a discussion of Dignāga's philosophy of language—the *apoha* theory—where the term "*adarśanamātra*" is used to state that the negative concomitance (*vyatireka*) can be determined on the basis of mere non-perception (*adarśanamātreṇa*). This could be the basis on which Īśvarasena developed his own concept of mere non-perception. The second passage, on the other hand, contains the term *anupalabdhi*, which was later commonly used by Dharmakīrti. This passage, in turn, is referred to and discussed at length in Dharmakīrti's *Pramāṇavārttika-svavṛtti*.

It seems that no further progress has been made to trace pre-Dharmakīrti sources on non-cognition, although, as pointed out by Steinkellner (1992: 403

n27), there is a strong need for such a study. Somewhat surprisingly, little attention has been paid to the many extant Chinese sources that make mention of the three *pramāṇa*s. The predominance of three *pramāṇa*s in China owes to the influence of pre-Dignāga works on Buddhist logic. These works, attributed to Maitreyanātha, Asaṅga, or Vasubandhu, usually admit more than two *pramāṇa*s, the third of which, however, is given as *āgama* or *śabda*. When Xuanzang and others introduced Dignāga's works on logic to China in the seventh century, scholars started to realize that *āgama* or *śabda* should not stand out as an independent *pramāṇa*. Thus, there was a movement to recognize only two kinds of *pramāṇa*s, and this position can be seen, most naturally, in the commentarial tradition of Dignāga's works.

But soon after or around this time, a new set of three *pramāṇa*s emerged. In this set, besides the usual members of perception and inference, we find a third one called *feiliang*, or literally non-*pramāṇa*. Even without looking closely at the details, one might suspect that this third *pramāṇa* is related to Īśvarasena's ideas. We are thus given a gleam of hope that we may be able to find the traces of this lost tradition.

5.2 *Feiliang*

As a *pramāṇa* that is listed together with perception and inference, *feiliang* needs some explanation. *Fei* (非) denotes a sense of negation, meaning "no" or "non-"; *liang* (量) literally means "to measure" and is used to translate the Sanskrit term *pramāṇa*, which is a technical term in Buddhist epistemology and logic. When used in a nontechnical sense, *feiliang* means immeasurable or unlimited, and its Sanskrit equivalent is *apramāṇa*. Even in its technical usage, the term "*feiliang*" could have two meanings. The first simply indicates a negation of being a *pramāṇa*, thus meaning "not a *pramāṇa*," and its Sanskrit equivalent is also *apramāṇa*. This usage is frequently seen in the works of

Dharmakīrti; for instance, in the *Pramāṇavārttika* (PV) II.89, III.335, IV.3, and IV.237 (according to Miyasaka [1971–72]).

The other meaning of *feiliang* is found in the sources that we will discuss in the section titled "Non-cognition as the Third *Pramāṇa*," where it is listed as a third *pramāṇa* over and above perception and inference. At this point, we cannot be sure about its Sanskrit equivalent, as most of the sources for this usage are only extant in Chinese. As a matter of fact, Buddhist scholars in East Asia have never attempted to make a connection between this concept and its likely Indian sources, and have instead followed the traditional view of Kuiji, who defines *feiliang* in terms of pseudo-perception (*pratyakṣābhāsa*) and pseudo-inference (*anumānābhāsa*).

Pseudo-perception here refers to those types of cognition, such as recollection, erroneous cognition, desire, and so on, that are not considered valid means of knowledge, but appear only as perceptions (*pratyakṣa-ābhāsa*). Post-Dignāga commentators led extensive discussions on the causes of pseudo-perception; some held that it is due to the interference of mental consciousness, which is capable of conceptual construction, in the functioning of the sense consciousness, while others saw it to be caused by defects in the sense organs themselves (Chu 2004: 113–15). Pseudo-inference refers to an inference that violates the rules for proper inference. Both pseudo-perception and pseudo-inference are considered erroneous, and thus called *feiliang*—non-*pramāṇa* or not a *pramāṇa*. "Non-" or "not" here implies a sense of "not being (a proper *x*)" or "mistaken."

But this understanding is not applicable to *feiliang* when it is listed as one of the three *pramāṇa*s, where it is considered a valid means of knowledge rather than a mistaken cognition. More importantly, in Sanskrit and Tibetan sources, we do not find a concept like non-*pramāṇa* that covers the scope of pseudo-perception and pseudo-inference and is listed as a third *pramāṇa*. It is true that in the Śaṅkarasvāmin's *Nyāyapraveśa*, pseudo-perception and pseudo-inference are listed almost immediately after perception and inference have been defined.[4] In his commentary on this very text, Kuiji elaborates the view that both pseudo-perception and pseudo-inference are included under the concept of *feiliang*, which is therefore understood to be parallel to perception and inference. He says: "Both pseudo-perception and pseudo-inference are covered by *feiliang*. Therefore, perception is included in neither inference nor *feiliang*, and inference is not included in *feiliang* either."[5]

Although Kuiji offered us the most explicit definition of *feiliang*, one that came to dominate the later history of East Asian Buddhism, he was not the first one to come up with this concept. One of the sources he relied on could have been the **Vijñaptimātratāsiddhi*, a collection of commentaries on Vasubandhu's *Triṃśikā* by ten Indian scholars, including Dharmapāla. In this text, the term "*feiliang*" appears thrice in the context of a discussion of Dharmapāla's theory of the four divisions of cognition. When arguing that the cognition of self-cognition (**svasaṃvittisaṃvitti*) has to be established in addition to the other three divisions of cognition, namely, self-cognition (*svasaṃvedana*), the seeing portion (*darśana*), and the seen portion (*nimitta*), Dharmapāla mentions the term "*feiliang*."[6] Here, the term "*feiliang*" appears in the same context as perception and inference, which, as is held by Kuiji and other commentators, implies the parallel status of the three. At the same time, they understood *feiliang* to be pseudo-perception and pseudo-inference, both of which are listed immediately after the definitions of the two *pramāṇas* in the *Nyāyapraveśa*. As a result, we have a list of three parallel *pramāṇas*: perception, inference, and *feiliang*.

On careful examination of the commentarial work in this area in seventh- or eighth-century China, we can detect a complex that comprises of at least three different, possibly independent Indian sources. A subtle synthesis of the three contributed to the formation of a rather unique concept of *feiliang* among East Asian Buddhists. These three sources are: (1) Śaṅkarasvāmin's emphasis on pseudo-perception and pseudo-inference, both of which are listed immediately after the definitions of perception and inference; (2) Dharmapāla's concept of *feiliang* and its possible parallel status to the two *pramāṇas*; (3) the proposal, from an unknown origin, of a third *pramāṇa*, which is called *feiliang*.

The third of these sources, as we assumed earlier, might have to do with Īśvarasena's concept of *adarśanamātra* or *upalabdhyabhāvamātra*. If this is the case, "*fei*" in the concept *feiliang* should not mean "not being (a proper *x*)" or "mistaken." Rather, it should be understood literally as "absence" or "non-occurrence (of *x*)." *Feiliang* therefore would come to mean the absence of *pramāṇa* or non-cognition—very close to the concept proposed by Īśvarasena.

5.3 *Apramāṇatā (Apramāṇatva)*

As none of Īśvarasena's works are extant today, we cannot prove our assumption with any "direct" evidence. But his views were introduced and criticized in some of the works of Dharmakīrti, and it is likely that these criticisms, in addition to a partial integration of his views, eventually came to inform Dharmakīrti's own theory of non-cognition (*anupalabdhi*). Dharmakīrti's criticism of Īśvarasena's view of non-cognition is found mainly in verses 198–212 of the *Pramāṇavārttikasvavṛtti*, which have been translated and studied by Yaita (1984, 1985a, b). The development of Dharmakīrti's theory is divided by Kellner (2003) into three main steps, which are indicated respectively by three different groups of texts. Her study carefully analyses each stage of the development, and remains the most comprehensive study of Dharmakīrti's theory of non-cognition.

Nevertheless, both scholars (and, for that matter, all contemporary scholars) neglected another important section of the PV, namely, verses 85–100 of the *pratyakṣa* chapter. The importance of this passage lies in the fact that the terms "*apramāṇatva*" and "*apramāṇatā*" are used on several occasions. In various other places in the PV, these terms mean "not-a-*pramāṇa*-ness," based on *apramāṇa* in the meaning of "not a *pramāṇa*." In this section, however, they seem to refer to some kind of "non-cognition-ness."[7]

According to Tosaki (1979), the section PV III.85–100 focuses on the issue of negative inferential cognition within the context of a discussion about the number of *pramāṇa*s, where Dharmakīrti criticizes the view that there is only one means of knowledge, that is, perception, and also the view that there are more than two *pramāṇa*s. Being a follower of Dignāga, he refutes these views mainly by arguing for the validity of inference as a means of knowledge. But does Dharmakīrti yield any information about his teacher Īśvarasena's theory of the third *pramāṇa* while he discusses negative inferential cognition in the context of the enumeration of *pramāṇa*s?

In this section, Dharmakīrti states, first of all, that "negation (*pratiṣedha*) is in all cases established through non-cognition (*anupalambhataḥ*)."[8] In order to arrive at a negatively phrased conclusion through an inference, one proceeds through the following steps: "Whatever [affirmative] statement of something contradictory [to the negandum] or of [something contradictory to] its cause is found in a negative inference, implies the non-cognition (*apramāṇatva*) of that [negandum]."[9] For instance, if someone feels cold, it implies that he or she does not sense fire, and therefore the existence of fire is negated. Similarly, trembling also implies that one does not sense fire, because trembling is caused by coldness. As a result, the existence of fire is negated, as shown in the following diagram:

nonexistence of A (fire)
↑
existence of B (coldness or trembling) → non-cognition of A (fire)

For those who are accustomed to the Western way of logical thinking, the nonexistence of A (fire) can be inferred directly from the existence of B (coldness or trembling) without the intermediary non-cognition of A (fire). This is because fire is contradictory to coldness and its effect (i.e., trembling), so they cannot coexist with each other. But according to Dharmakīrti, their contradiction or impossibility of coexistence has not been proved yet, and cannot act as the basis for proper inference. The non-cognition of A is a necessary step for inferring the nonexistence of A from the existence of B. This is why Dharmakīrti holds that all negative inferences are established through non-cognition. In other words, non-cognition is "the prover (*prasādhikā*) of nonexistence (*abhāva*)."[10] He further remarks that this point is so obvious that even an ignorant cowherd could understand it: "We say that the very absence of cognizing (*apramāṇatā*) a thing is a mark (*liṅga*) of its absence. This [needs to be explicitly stated] only for very stupid people, as it should be clear even to a cowherd."[11]

What interests us here most is the usage of *apramāṇatva* or *apramāṇatā*. It is evident that both are used interchangeably with *anupalabdhi* or *anupalambha*, all meaning "non-cognition." In his *Pramāṇavāttikavṛtti* (PVV), Manorathanandin explicitly treats *apramāṇatā*, *pramāṇarahitatā* (absence of *pramāṇa*), and *anupalabdhi* as synonyms, stating: "Whatever is non-perception (*adarśana*), that is non-cognitionness (*apramāṇatā*), absence of *pramāṇa* (*pramāṇarahitatā*), and non-cognition (*anupalabdhi*)."[12] Moreover, he explains *apramāṇatva* in terms of the absence of *pramāṇa* (*pramāṇarahitatā*), and *apramāṇatā* in terms of the non-operation of *pramāṇa* (*pramāṇanivṛtti*).[13]

If the concept *feiliang* in Chinese sources has to do with the *apramāṇatva* or *apramāṇatā* as used by Dharmakīrti in this section, then it may also be interpreted as the absence of *pramāṇa*, the non-operation of *pramāṇa*, or non-cognition (*anupalabdhi*), and its Sanskrit equivalent could thus be *apramāṇatva* or *apramāṇatā*. As the concept *feiliang* is discussed in the context of a theory that proposes the third *pramāṇa* non-cognition over and above perception and inference, we can assume that *apramāṇatva* or *apramāṇatā* in Dharmakīrti's usage was adopted from Īśvarasena, who is evidently the only one upholding such a theory. Sources from Dharmakīrti thus can serve as indirect evidence for the relationship between the Īśvarasena tradition and relevant Chinese sources.

5.4 Non-cognition and Nonexistence

In Dharmakīrti's discussion on *apramāṇatva* or *apramāṇatā*, an important feature is that it functions as the "prover" (*prasādhikā*) of nonexistence. He then goes on to stress that this principle only applies to perceptible things (*dṛśya*). Their absence is proved if and only if they are not perceived when all the conditions for perception are sufficient. As for imperceptible things (*adṛśya*), such as ghosts (*piśāca*), their non-perception or non-cognition cannot determine whether they exist or not. In his view, non-cognition (*apramāṇatā*) is the non-perception (*darśanābhāva*) of the perceptible (*dṛśyasya*),[14] as he says: "We have already shown that non-cognition of this sort [of super-sensory objects] decides nothing. Thus in regard to absolutely invisible things, one cannot determine whether they exist or not."[15]

To distinguish objects of non-cognition into the perceptible and imperceptible is one of the innovative contributions of Dharmakīrti. It is on the basis of this point that he criticizes his teacher Īśvarasena for taking non-cognition to be an independent means of knowledge regardless of the status of its object. To my knowledge, such an explicit distinction is not found in the works of any pre-Dharmakīrti thinkers. Dignāga, for instance, never distinguished perceptible and imperceptible objects of non-cognition when discussing the concepts of *anupalabdhi* or *adarśanamātra*. Instead, the object of non-cognition under discussion is usually imperceptible by nature, for instance, the Sāṅkhya concept of "primordial matter" (*pradhāna*) that he refutes in the *Nyāyamukha*, or the words (*śabda*) in the *Pramāṇasamuccaya*. In the eyes of Dharmakīrti, however, the non-cognition of the primordial matter does not in itself prove its nonexistence. Dignāga himself probably realized this problem, and in a later work, the *Pramāṇasamuccayavṛtti*, we find this statement regarding the non-cognition of the primordial matter had been excluded.[16]

As a matter of fact, in many pre-Dharmakīrti texts, non-cognition or *anupalabdhi* simply stands for nonexistence. This fact even inspired Lamotte to attempt to render the term "*anupalabdhi*" as "nonexistence" (Steinkellner 1992: 398–9). Steinkellner, who disagreed with his proposal, singled out a few examples that suggest a line of thought similar to that followed by Dharmakīrti, namely, that the object of non-cognition is not simply nonexistent, but resides in the "middle way" between existence and nonexistence (410). This observation particularly makes sense when considering the so-called positive Buddhist concepts of *nirvāṇa*, *prajñā*, *śūnyatā*, and so on. For instance, it is repeatedly stressed that "*prajñā* is non-cognizable" in the Perfection of Wisdom literature. This does not mean that *prajñā* does not exist, but that it is rather beyond the reach of words and thought, and thus non-cognizable to the conventional mind.

In the case of those concepts or views that Buddhists deny, however, non-cognition becomes the only basis for negating them. Dignāga's argument against the Sāṅkhya concept of primordial matter (*pradhāna*), which we mentioned earlier, is such an example. Another example is found in Asaṅga's **Madhyamakānusāra*. When explaining the reason for Nāgārjuna's argument against the Sarvāstivāda view that space exists, Asaṅga says: "Space is ultimately something non-cognizable (*bukede* 不可得, **anupalabdhi*), just like a rabbit's horn that, in the end, cannot be cognized by any of the six senses. Space is also non-cognizable in the same way, therefore it is known that [space] does not exist."[17] The Chinese term "*bukede*" here can be reconstructed into Sanskrit as *anupalabdhi*, the word used frequently by Dharmakīrti and on a few occasions by Dignāga, as it is evident that this Chinese word was consistently used to translate *anupalabdhi* in Dignāga's texts or *nopalabhyate* in the Perfection of Wisdom literature. Here, Asaṅga clearly defines *anupalabdhi* as implying "non-cognizable by the six senses," which include not only the five sensory organs, but also the mind. Therefore, *anupalabdhi* here should be understood as "non-cognition" rather than "non-perception." It is exactly through the non-cognition that one *knows* the absence of space or a rabbit's horn. The rabbit's horn, according to Kumārila's classification, belongs to "absolute nonexistence" (*atyantābhāva*), one of the four types of nonexistence.[18] For Asaṅga, space also belongs to this category. The non-cognition of both space and a rabbit's horn, in Dharmakīrti's understanding, is the non-cognition of the imperceptible (*adṛśyānupalabdhi*), and thus cannot decide their absence. But for Asaṅga, this non-cognition *knows* exactly their absence, and it is a definite way to acquire knowledge with regard to the absence of something.

Interestingly enough, in the **Buddhadhātuśāstra*, a work attributed to Vasubandhu, a similar argument is attributed to an opponent to refute the existence of the reality body (*dharmakāya*). The opponent argues:

> The *dharmakāya* is definitely nonexistent, because it cannot be cognized. If a thing cannot be cognized by any of the six forms of consciousness, then it is definitely nonexistent. This is like a rabbit's horn that cannot be cognized by any of the six forms of consciousness and thus does not exist. The same is true for the *dharmakāya*. Therefore it is definitely nonexistent.[19]

Here the basic reason for the denial of the existence of the *dharmakāya* is that it cannot be cognized by the five sense consciousnesses and mental consciousness. The rabbit's horn, being in absolute nonexistence, exemplifies the nonexistence of the *dharmakāya*. According to Buddhist teachings, however, the *dharmakāya* must be something existent, for otherwise many foundational Buddhist doctrines would not stand. Vasubandhu attempts to prove the existence of the *dharmakāya* by facing the challenge of this argument from non-cognition. He replies:

> You hold that the *dharmakāya* is nonexistent because it cannot be cognized by any of the six forms of consciousness. This is not correct. Why? One can

> realize *nirvāṇa* through a skillful means (*upāya*). An *upāya* is thus named because it corresponds to right action. The *dharmakāya* is known through this *upāya*, just like the transcendental mind of the noble can be cognized by the [supernatural power] of knowing others' minds.[20]

What interests us here is that Vasubandhu does not challenge the argument from non-cognition itself as does Dharmakīrti, but instead tries to prove that the *dharmakāya* can be cognized through a certain kind of *upāya* just as the transcendental mind is known through the supernatural ability of knowing others' minds. His emphasis on the "cognizability" of the *dharmakāya*, ironically, strengthens the presupposition made by the opponent's argument from non-cognition, namely, that the cognizable is existent, while the non-cognizable is nonexistent.

A similar view to that of Vasubandhu's opponent is found in the **Mahāyā nasaṃgrahaṭīkā* (MSṬ) of Asvabhāva.[21] According to its Chinese translation, this text appears to be the first to use the term "*feiliang*" in the sense of non-cognition. It says: "'Like they appear, [they] do not exist.' [This means:] Self, *dharma*, grasper and grasped do not exist in reality because [they are] cognized by non-cognition (*feiliang*), so [they are] regarded as nonexistent."[22] According to the Yogācāra teachings, grasper, grasped, self, and *dharma* are considered illusory, and thus do not really exist. Asvabhāva adds something new to this statement by utilizing the epistemologically oriented concept "non-cognition" to explain their nonexistence via a method similar to that of Asaṅga and Vasubandhu's "opponent." Importantly, the fact that *feiliang* or *tshad ma med pa* is used here in the sense of non-cognition further corresponds with Dharmakīrti's using *apramāṇatā* or *apramāṇatva* interchangeably with *anupalabdhi*. Elsewhere in the text, Asvabhāva indicates a similar caution to Dharmakīrti, that is, something's being non-cognizable does not necessarily confirm its nonexistence. He says: "Therefore, here '*ālambana* is non-cognizable' only means that [*ālambana*] is not fully apprehensible, not nonexistent. For it is not the case that nothing exists, rather, something exists but is not fully apprehensible."[23] *Ālambana*, or object of cognition according to the Yogācāra teachings, cannot be completely nonexistent; therefore, the discussion on the non-cognition of *ālambana* could only yield an ambiguous result.

As we see, authors such as Asaṅga, Vasubandhu, Dignāga, and Asvabhāva take very different views from that of Dharmakīrti with regard to the relationship between non-cognition and nonexistence. The former holds that the non-operation of sensory and mental consciousnesses, that is, non-cognition, may determine or "know" the absence of things, both perceptible and imperceptible, which include abstract metaphysical entities. Dharmakīrti, on the other hand, holds that non-cognition can only determine the absence of the perceptible, but not of the imperceptible. Detailed discussions in the works of Dharmakīrti, in addition to the ambiguous attitude of Dignāga and Asvabhāva on this issue, seem to suggest that Dharmakīrti's view, which is later historically, is more powerful in resolving the issue.

5.5 Non-cognition as the Third *Pramāṇa*

Returning to Īśvarasena's views on the subject, another source that may have been influenced by his theories is Jinaputra et al.'s commentary on YBh. In a passage discussing the relationship between various kinds of consciousnesses and different *pramāṇas*, this commentary states: "The five [sense] consciousnesses are grouped together and explained first because they are all included under perception, whereas the other consciousnesses [i.e., mental consciousness, *manas*, and *ālaya* consciousness] are uncertain, for they can be included under perception, inference or non-cognition (*feiliang*). So they are grouped separately and explained secondly."[24] As a commentator of a foundational Yogācāra text, Jinaputra et al. are, however, concerned with the relationship between consciousness and *pramāṇa*, which implies that they have been influenced by Dignāga and his school. More importantly, it seems that they admit the third *pramāṇa* non-cognition in addition to perception and inference. Although they do not clearly define non-cognition (*feiliang*), they have explicitly listed it immediately after the two *pramāṇas*. With the support of evidence found in the works of Dharmakīrti and Asvabhāva, we can count this passage as another piece of evidence for Īśvarasena's paradigm of three *pramāṇas*.

Reexamining the passage from the **Vijñaptimātratāsiddhi* that was elaborated extensively by Kuiji and his followers, we can now see the possibility of an alternative interpretation. If we disregard Kuiji's interpretation of *feiliang* as implying pseudo-perception and pseudo-inference and render *feiliang* literally as non-cognition, then this passage by Dharmapāla would be another source that lists non-cognition immediately after perception and inference, thus revealing another link to Īśvarasena's theory of three *pramāṇas*. As a matter of fact, this alternative interpretation can be found in Chinese commentarial works of the seventh and eighth centuries, and it is only because of the dominant influence of Kuiji and his followers that this position came to be neglected by subsequent scholars. One of the figures who upheld such a view was Dunnyun, a Korean monk in Chang'an (長安). In his commentary on YBh, he says:

> There are five arguments to refute the existence of atoms (*paramāṇu*). First, if it is observed that atoms are not cognized by various *pramāṇas* such as perception and inference, then they are certainly nonexistent, just like a rabbit's horn. Although the opponent holds that they are cognizable by perception, the proponent thinks that they are known by non-cognition (*feiliang*). Perception can only perceive the visual object (*rūpa*) beyond the level of molecules (*aṇu*). Atoms, accordingly, are not [above this level].[25]

His view comes very close to that of Asvabhāva, except that for him non-cognition knows the absence of external objects such as atoms rather than metaphysical entities such as self or *dharma*.

Another example of this alternative interpretation of *feiliang* can be found in the writings of Tankuang (曇曠), an eighth-century monk-scholar who became known to us only after the discovery of the Dunhuang (敦煌) manuscripts in the early twentieth century. In the following passage, he offers a clear definition of the third *pramāṇa* called non-cognition (*feiliang*):

> There are three types of *pramāṇa* that correspond to eight kinds of consciousnesses. The first is the *pramāṇa* of perception (**pratyakṣapramāṇa*). Perception is meant [to perceive] what is present; *pramāṇa* is what measures. That which is devoid of the conceptual construction of names and genres, and can know non-erroneously the vividly present visual object (*rūpa*) etc. as clearly as looking into a mirror, is called perception. Perception is *pramāṇa*; "*pratyakṣapramāṇa*" is a *karmadhāraya* compound.
>
> The second is the *pramāṇa* of inference (**anumānapramāṇa*). Inference means to infer from similar cases; *pramāṇa*'s meaning is identical to [that given] before. The right knowledge that arises from the various characteristics of what is perceived, and knows the size or impermanence of the object that is not present, is inference. Inference is *pramāṇa*; "*anumānapramāṇa*" is also a *karmadhāraya* compound.
>
> The third is non-cognition (*feiliang*). If an object cannot be clearly perceived, nor can it be inferred on various grounds, it is actually nonexistent and non-cognizable. That which knows the non-cognizable is called non-cognition (*feiliang*). It therefore cannot be interpreted as any of the six types of compounds.[26]

Here *feiliang* is explicitly defined as "that which knows the non-cognizable and the nonexistent," and as the third *pramāṇa* over and above perception and inference. Elsewhere, Tankuang discusses the object of each *pramāṇa*. He says: "The awareness (*jñāna*) attained after [liberation] embraces three kinds of *pramāṇa*: that which takes particulars as object is the awareness called perception; that which takes universals as object is the awareness called inference; that which takes the past and the future as object is the awareness called non-cognition (*feiliang*)."[27] Buddhist scholars after Dignāga commonly held the view that particulars and universals are the objects of perception and inference respectively. What about the object of the third *pramāṇa* non-cognition? According to our earlier discussion, it seems to be nonexistence. But why does Tankuang say that non-cognition takes the past and the future as object? If we recall Kumārila's fourfold classification of nonexistence, namely, prior nonexistence (*prāgabhāva*), posterior nonexistence (*dhvaṃsa*), mutual nonexistence (*anyonyābhāva*), and absolute nonexistence (*atyantābhāva*), we will realize that the past and the future here refer to the first two types of nonexistence. Therefore, Tankuang does not contradict himself: non-cognition still takes nonexistence as its object.

Among the aforementioned references to the notion of non-cognition from the works of Asaṅga, Vasubandhu, Dignāga, Asvabhāva, Jinaputra et al., Dharmapāla, and Dharmakīrti, the term "*feiliang*" or "*apramāṇatā*" (*apramāṇatva*) in the sense of non-cognition appears only in the works of the last four authors. This may imply that these scholars took non-cognition (*anupalabdhi*) as an independent *pramāṇa* that was called, ironically, *a-pramāṇatā* or *a-pramāṇatva*. It also appears that they did not do so at their will; at least we know that Dharmakīrti opposed such an idea. Hypothetically, as an explanation for this discrepancy, we may propose the following: these scholars were exposed to what was at that time an influential theory, and some simply followed it, while others attacked it. This "influential theory" was Īśvarasena's paradigm of three *pramāṇa*s, the third being *adarśanamātra* or *apramāṇatā* (*apramāṇatva*).

On the Chinese side, Kuiji's understanding *feiliang* as pseudo-perception and pseudo-inference, and his listing it side by side with perception and inference, probably conformed to a classification by Śaṅkarasvāmin, who put the four in the same list. Tankuang, on the other hand, explicitly understood *feiliang* to mean "non-cognition," and took it to be a third *pramāṇa* over and above perception and inference. It is evident that Tankuang and other Yogācāra scholars active in the Dunhuang area at the time were associated with the tradition of the Ximing (西明) temple, whose leading voice was the Korean monk Wŏnch'ŭk (圓測). Owing to a lack of textual sources, however, we do not have any evidence supporting the assertion that he holds the same view as that of Tankuang on the issue of *feiliang*. At least, in the eyes of Kuiji's followers, this issue was not a focal point for the debates between the Ci'en (慈恩) and Ximing schools. We are also unable to determine the actual source from which Tankuang developed a view on *feiliang* that differed from that of Kuiji, but came very close to the concept non-cognition as expounded by Indian scholars such as Asvabhāva, Jinaputra et al., and Dharmakīrti, and most importantly confirmed Īśvarasena's theory of three *pramāṇas*.[28] Tankuang's works offer us the most convincing evidence that Īśvarasena's theory of three *pramāṇas* left some traces in the history of Chinese Buddhism, despite the fact that we cannot determine with certainty the actual channel for such diffusion.

6

Empty Terms

The problem of empty terms—expressions that are meaningful but do not refer to anything existent—is one of the focal issues in analytic philosophy. Russell's theory of descriptions, a proposal attempting to solve this problem, attracted much attention and is considered a hallmark of the analytic tradition. Scholars of Indian and Buddhist philosophy, for instance, McDermott (1970), Shaw (1974), Perszyk (1984), and Matilal (1985), have studied discussions of empty terms in Indian and Buddhist philosophy. But most of these studies rely heavily on the Nyāya or Navya-Nyāya sources, in which Buddhists are portrayed as opponents to be defeated, and thus do not truly reflect Buddhist views on this issue.

The present chapter will explore how Dignāga, the founder of Buddhist logic, deals with the issue of empty terms, and it will do so by analysis of his original works. His approach is subtle and complicated. On the one hand, he proposes a method of paraphrase that resembles Russell's theory of descriptions. On the other, by relying on his philosophy of language—the *apoha* theory—he tends to fall into a pan-fictionalism. Through the efforts of his follower Dharmakīrti, the latter approach would become more acceptable among Indian and Tibetan Buddhists.

Dignāga's work also had its Chinese commentators, who, free from the influence of Dharmakīrti, dealt with the empty term issue in three ways: (1) by adhering to Dignāga's method of paraphrase; (2) by allowing exceptions for non-implicative negation; and (3) by indicating the propositional attitude of a given proposition. Among these, the third proved the most popular.

6.1 "Primordial Matter Does Not Exist"

Many basic doctrines of Buddhist philosophy can be stated as negative existential propositions. For instance, "no-self" (*anātman*) means "the self does not exist"; "impermanence" (*anitya*) means "a permanent entity does not exist"; "emptiness" (*śūnyatā*) means "intrinsic nature does not exist" (*niḥsvabhāvatā*). The subjects of these propositions are all considered empty terms because, as stated in the propositions themselves, they do not really exist. Therefore, the Buddhist tradition has had to face the problem of empty subject terms from its very inception.

Even though the problem of empty subjects was embedded in the tradition itself, it was not treated in any systematic way until the development of Buddhist logic in the sixth century. Later treatments of this problem usually rely on the following passage from Dignāga's early work, *Nyāyamukha*:

> [Question:] But suppose that we are to prove [not a property but] a subject (*dharmin*, property-possessor) to be existent or nonexistent. For example, some [i.e., the Sāṅkhyas] argue:
>
> [Thesis] Primordial matter (*pradhāna*) exists.
>
> [Reason] Because we see that the various individuals possess a [similar] general characteristic.
>
> While some others [i.e., the Buddhists] argue:
>
> [Thesis] Primordial matter does not exist.
>
> [Reason] Because there is non-apprehension of it.
>
> (*na santi pradhānādayo 'nupalabdheḥ*)
>
> How do you explain this?

> [Answer:] [As for the first inference,] the thesis should be formulated as "The various individuals certainly possess one and the same cause [i.e., primordial matter]," but they do not prove [directly the existence of] primordial matter [i.e., the subject]; hence, there is no error [of proving the subject of the thesis with the reason].
>
> [As for the second inference,] when they argue that [primordial matter] does not exist [because of non-apprehension], "non-apprehension" is a property of the imagined concept [i.e., primordial matter] (*kalpitasyānupalabdhir dharmaḥ*); hence, there is also no error of [proving] the subject of the thesis [with the reason].[1]

Here Dignāga deals with two types of propositions: (1) a positive existential one, "primordial matter exists"; and (2) a negative existential one, "primordial matter does not exist." The subject "primordial matter" is a metaphysical concept developed among the Sāṅkhyas to signify the first cause in their cosmological system. The Buddhists, however, do not accept a first cause and hence regard "primordial matter" as an empty term. Discussions of these positive and negative existential propositions thus reflect Buddhist ways of dealing with empty subject terms. I classify these into four approaches: (1) the method of paraphrase; (2) the principle of conceptual subjects; (3) the distinguishing of two types of negation; and (4) the principle of propositional attitude.

The first two approaches have been discussed by Tillemans (1999: 171–85), who suggests that they can be traced back to the passage cited earlier and that they were both used by Indian Buddhist scholars such as Dharmakīrti and Prajñākaragupta. But in later Indian and Tibetan Buddhism, the dominant approach to the problem of empty terms combined the principle of conceptual subjects with the theory of exclusion (*apoha*). In the meantime, distinguishing between two types of negation was used to deal with negative existential propositions having an empty term as their subject. Although it entails certain difficulties, this approach can be seen in the work of authors such as Kamalaśīla, Tsong kha pa, and Huizhao.[2] The principle of propositional attitude, however, was popular among Chinese Buddhist scholars. All four methods had a complicated history of development in their respective traditions, which I am not going to discuss in detail. Instead, I will mainly demonstrate how each is applied to the problem of empty subject terms and their philosophical significance.

6.2 The Method of Paraphrase

What Tillemans (1999: 174) calls "the method of paraphrase," developed in sixth-century India, shares many attributes with Russell's theory of descriptions. The key to Russell's theory is distinguishing between logical and grammatical structures. The grammatical subject of a statement may not be its logical subject. For instance, "the present king of France" is the grammatical subject in the sentence "The present king of France is bald," but cannot be its logical subject; otherwise, it will run into the problem of empty subject term because presently there is no king of France. Its logical structure is revealed when paraphrased as "There is one and only one entity which has the property of being king of France, and this entity is bald," or in symbolic form as "$\exists x[(Kx \,\&\, \forall y(Ky \rightarrow x=y)) \,\&\, Bx]$." In this Russellean translation, the subject position is occupied by what is known as a "bound variable" or "variable of quantification," for example, words like "something," "nothing," or "everything." Thus, the burden of objective reference is thrown upon the shoulder of the bound variable, which does not purport to name, but refers to entities generally (Matilal 1985: 85). Therefore, we can avoid unwanted metaphysical commitments to nonexistent objects; meanwhile, we can freely employ sentences using expressions that fail to denote.

The Dignāga passage given earlier contains the earliest form of the method of paraphrase found in extant Buddhist sources. For Buddhists who do not accept the first cause, the statement "primordial matter exists" is a proposition with an empty subject term, and hence meaningless. If, however, it is paraphrased as "The various individuals certainly possess one and the same cause," then the logical subject is "the various individuals" rather than "primordial matter," and the empty subject term is avoided. In his later work *Pramāṇasamuccaya*, Dignāga made a similar statement regarding this positive existential proposition:

> [Question:] Some [i.e., the Sāṅkhyas] argue:
>
> [Thesis] Unique primordial matter exists.
>
> [Reason] Because we see that the various individuals possess a [similar] general characteristic.
>
> How do you explain this?
>
> [Answer:] They should formulate the thesis as "The various individuals certainly possess one and the same cause [i.e., primordial matter]," and the example is "just like the pieces of a thing possess one and the same cause."[3]

Based on this statement, we can reconstruct a valid inference that avoids the empty subject term by means of paraphrase:

(D1) [Thesis] The various individuals certainly possess one and the same cause.
[Reason] Because we see that the various individuals possess a similar general characteristic.
[Example] Just like the pieces of a thing possess one and the same cause.

Tillemans (1999: 177–80) singled out other instances employing the same method to deal with empty subject terms in Dharmakīrti's PV IV.141–2 and 144–5 and their commentaries by Prajñākaragupta. These instances, however, do not closely follow Dignāga's classical cases. In Shentai's commentary on the *Nyāyamukha*—the only extant complete commentary on this work—he further explains how Dignāga's method of paraphrase is used to deal not only with positive existential propositions, but also negative ones.[4]

Shentai first of all explains that "the various individuals" refers to the twenty-three kinds of entities, which, along with the transcendental spirit (*puruṣa*) and primordial matter (*pradhāna*), constitute the twenty-five entities in the Sāṅkhya doctrinal system. In this system, the twenty-three are believed to possess a cause, which is primordial matter. Taking "the twenty-three individuals" as its logical subject, Shentai paraphrases the positive proposition as the following inference:

> (S1) Thesis: Here the twenty-three individuals certainly possess one and the same cause.
> Reason: Because they are various individuals.
> Similar Example: Just like multiple slips of white sandalwood.[5]

S1 is only slightly different from D1; both exemplify the method of paraphrase used by Buddhist scholars to deal with such positive propositions. Regarding the negative existential proposition "primordial matter does not exist," Shentai offered two solutions. One is to indicate the propositional attitude, which I will discuss later in S3; the other is to reconstruct the logical structure as follows:

> (S2) Thesis: The twenty-three individuals do not possess primordial matter as their cause.
> Reason: Because primordial matter cannot be apprehended.
> Similar Example: Just like a rabbit's horn.[6]

As in the case of S1, the empty term "primordial matter" in S2 is replaced by "the twenty-three individuals," which acts as its logical subject. But the reason or minor premise in S2 still takes the empty term "primordial matter" as its subject. Shentai did not replace it with "the twenty-three individuals," for we cannot say "the twenty-three individuals cannot be apprehended." This may be because the method of paraphrase works only with a single proposition, but not necessarily with the whole inference. This might be a reason why Dignāga himself did not explore further in this direction. As we will see in this chapter, in his later work *Pramāṇasamuccaya*, he simply avoided any discussion of this negative existential proposition.

Unlike the relative influence enjoyed by the theory of descriptions in the West, the method of paraphrase did not attract much attention in the Buddhist tradition. We have discussed here a few instances found in the Indian and Chinese sources. The entire Tibetan tradition seems devoid of any traces of this method, but not because the problem of empty subject terms was not taken seriously in that tradition. On the contrary, since the Madhyamaka doctrine of emptiness and the logical system of Dignāga and Dharmakīrti were equally important for the dGe lugs pas, the dominant school in Tibetan Buddhism, the handling of empty terms was an urgent matter, and the concept of emptiness is itself usually expressed in a proposition with an empty subject term: "intrinsic nature does not exist." The Tibetan approach to the problem can be called the principle of conceptual subjects.

6.3 The Principle of Conceptual Subjects

As we know, Russell developed his theory of description partly in response to Meinong's theory of objects. According to that theory, things like "round-square" are nonexistent objects, which means that they are neither existences (*Existenz*) nor subsistences (*Bestand*), but their thus-being (*Sosein*) or character can still be referred to or discussed. This is because thus-being is independent of being (*Sein*) or existence. Russell instead held to a robust sense of realism by insisting that "entities should not be multiplied unnecessarily," and his theory of description would not work if it were not based on this sense of realism.

The method of paraphrase faced a difficult situation in the Buddhist tradition. The Buddhist logicians Dignāga and Dharmakīrti were committed to a nominalist view with regard to ontological issues (though their views had minor differences). They held that the particulars (*svalakṣaṇa*) perceived by the senses are real existents, while the universals (*sāmānyalakṣaṇa*) known by the mind are conceptual constructions. And conceptual constructions are made possible by the theory of excluding others (*anyāpoha*), according to which, a concept that has no real referent is established through the exclusion of other concepts. As a result, the so-called empty term "a rabbit's horn" shares the same ontological status with terms such as "desk" in the sense that both are believed to refer to certain verbal objects (*śabdārtha*). This is what Tillemans (1999: 174) calls the principle of conceptual subjects.

This principle yields a similar outcome as does the view of Meinong and his followers: it completely eliminates the problem of empty terms. According to this principle, there is no difference between empty and real terms; all of them are conceptual constructions. This view can be traced back to the passage of Dignāga cited earlier, which discusses the negative existential proposition of primordial matter. As mentioned earlier, in his later work *Pramāṇasamuccaya*, Dignāga excluded the passage on the negative proposition, retaining only the discussion of the positive proposition. This has generated much speculation. Katsura (1992: 231) and Tillemans (1999: 175) suggest that Dignāga in his later career simply adopted a more rigid attitude toward this issue, no longer admitting negative existential propositions with empty subject terms.

In any case, in Dharmakīrti's commentary, this passage was developed into the principle of conceptual subjects. Therein, the imagined concept (*kalpita*) means the verbal object (*śabdārtha*), which is the object of conceptual awareness (*kalpanājñāna*). The subject "primordial matter" signifies such a verbal object, and its property (*dharma*) "non-apprehension" (*anupalabdhi*) has this verbal object as basis. Thus, the reason "there is non-apprehension of it" does not rest on the failure of basis (*āśrayāsiddha*), a type of fallacy involving empty subject terms.[7] Taking "there is non-apprehension of primordial matter or of a rabbit's horn" as reason, we can reach the conclusion "primordial matter and a rabbit's horn do not exist." Neither proposition encounters the problem of empty subject terms, because their subjects can exist as an imagined concept or a verbal object. That they are claimed to be nonexistent in the conclusion is only because they do not have a basis in real existence (*bhāvānupādāne*), and hence cannot be perceived or apprehended (*anupalambhana*). It is not because they do not exist (*abhāva*) as imagined concepts.[8]

In the view of Russell, however, Dharmakīrti has to face the so-called Meinongian paradox: To say that the existent king of France does not exist is self-contradictory, and it is an inevitable weakness in Meinong's theory.[9] The Chinese commentator Huizhao points out the same difficulty: "If it is admitted that [primordial matter, i.e., a *dharmin*] exists, then it cannot be said to be nonexistent [i.e., having nonexistence as its property (*dharma*)]. This is self-contradictory."[10] This is because the subject "primordial matter" is assumed to exist, to be something of which properties can be predicated, and it would be self-contradictory if the predicate happened to be "nonexistent."[11] But for Dharmakīrti, this does not seem to be a problem. Although verbal objects are products of conceptual construction, some objects are real because of their causal efficacy (*arthakriyā*). Those which have no such causal efficacy, such as a rabbit's horn, are not real existents. It seems not self-contradictory to say, "A rabbit's horn exists as imagined concepts but is not real existent."

However, considering carefully the ontological implications of this position, we may recognize the danger of pan-fictionalism, where even fictional objects are considered existent. As a matter of fact, some Sarvāstivāda scholars explicitly classify things like a rabbit's horn or a turtle's hair as verbal existence (**śabdasat* or **nāmasat*, 名有), one of the five types of existence.[12] Since Dharmakīrti and his followers seldom discuss the typology of existence, we cannot be sure whether they would agree with such an ontological position.

In any case, the principle of conceptual subjects is not really a strictly technical method to deal with the problem of empty subject terms. Instead, it eliminates the problem by adopting an entirely different philosophical view. Tillemans

(1999: 181) once complained that the more technical method of paraphrase was less popular than the principle of conceptual subjects among Indian and Tibetan Buddhist scholars. I think this was because of the involvement of Mādhyamikas. In that tradition, propositions with empty subject terms are not incidental cases; rather, they effect its foundational doctrine of emptiness, and their problematic nature must be resolved. The Madhyamaka nominalist or even nihilist position and Dignāga's more technical theory of exclusion made the principle of conceptual subjects so influential in India and Tibet that the general attitude of Buddhists toward empty terms has been characterized as pan-fictionalism (Matilal 1985: 96).[13]

6.4 Two Types of Negation

In the Buddhist tradition, the issue of empty terms primarily involves the subjects of negative existential propositions, so the most effective solution has entailed distinguishing two different types of negation. Tillemans (1999: 173–4) has elided this distinction and the principle of conceptual subjects, though, in fact, distinguishing between types of negation is a more technically logical method that may stand independent of the principle of conceptual subjects. We will see this in operation in the case of Huizhao, to be discussed later. Indeed, the independence of these two methods may be seen in Tibetan discussions of empty subject terms; for example, A lag sha ngag dbang bstan dar begins his discussion of empty subjects with a criticism of distinguishing negative types before introducing the more powerful principle of conceptual subjects.[14]

The distinction at issue is between implicative negation (*paryudāsa*, *ma yin dgag*) and simple or non-implicative negation (*prasajya-pratiṣedha*, *med dgag*), and it can be traced back to the Grammarians, Dignāga, and Dharmakīrti. The Mādhayamika scholar Bhāviveka also discussed this distinction (Kajiyama 1973). Later scholars such as Prajñākaragupta, Kamalaśīla, Tsong kha pa, lCan skya ro pa'i rdo rje, A lag sha ngag dbang bstan dar, and Śākya mchog ldan applied the distinction to solve numerous cases of empty subject terms (Tillemans 1999: 173). Chinese Buddhist scholars were also familiar with Dignāga's distinction, which was rendered in Chinese as *zhequan* (遮詮; implicative negation) and *zhilan* (止濫; non-implicative negation).[15]

According to a definition given by the Grammarians, implicative negation "is a *paryudāsa* where the negative particle is construed [directly] with a following [substantive] word; in it affirmation is predominant and negation is subordinate."[16] It implicitly affirms a property while negating another, for instance, "John is unhappy." This type of negation is called "predicate term negation" or simply "term negation" in Aristotelian logic. Here, a negative predicate term ("unhappy") is affirmed of a subject. In contrast, non-implicative negation "is *prasajya-pratiṣedha* where the negative is construed [directly] with the verbal phrase; in it affirmation is subordinate and negation predominant."[17] It is a simple negation that does not imply any affirmation, for instance, "A rabbit's horn does not exist." This type of negation corresponds to the predicate denial in Aristotelian logic, and it is the strict sense of negation in which the operation of negation takes scope over the entire predication.

A lag sha ngag dbang bstan dar referred to a popular view attributed to Tsong kha pa and his followers that uses the distinction of these types of negation to solve the problem of empty subject terms. According to this view, even if the subject of thesis is a nonexistent entity (e.g., primordial matter), the fallacy of an unestablished basis of reason can be avoided, "so long as one presents simple negations (*med dgag; prasajyapratiṣedha*) as both the reason and property to be proved (*bsgrub bya'i chos; sādhyadharma*); but should one present a positive phenomenon (*sgrub pa; vidhi*) or an implicative negation (*ma yin dgag; paryudāsa*), it will then be an unestablished reason."[18] When discussing our current case "primordial matter does not exist," Huizhao expressed a similar view:

> A reason expressed with a negation that implies affirmation is a reason with existent basis, because it has to have an existent subject as its basis . . . [In contrast], its reason expressed with a negation that implies no affirmation is a reason with nonexistent basis, because it is taking the nonexistent [subject] as its basis, so it is not the case that [the reason] has an unestablished basis or a fallacy with regard to the subject.[19]

This solution is coincident to a general principle with regard to empty terms in Aristotelian logic, that is, "affirmation, with either positive or negative predicate terms, entail the existence of their subjects, while negations (predicate denials) do not" (Horn 1989: 103). It means that negation can be used to reject a presupposition of the existence of the subject. This is why negative existential propositions such as "a rabbit's horn does not exist" not only sound meaningful but are also true. The reason, according to Buddhist logicians, is that the negation here is a non-implicative one, for it does not imply the affirmation of anything while negating the existence of horns on rabbits. For cases like this, propositions with empty subject terms should be allowed. Otherwise, many statements of foundational Buddhist doctrines such as "the self does not exist" would become fallacious. In contrast, statements with implicative negation such as "a rabbit's horn is not sharp," which implies the affirmation of its bluntness, *are* fallacious. This way, the distinction between types of negation appears to have resolved the problem.

This approach, however, has its limitations. In the West, there are ongoing debates over whether and how the distinction between the internal or implicative negation and the external or non-implicative negation can tackle the presupposition of the existence of subject terms in semantic, classical logic, and multivalued logic (Horn 1989: 97–153). On the Buddhist side, A lag sha ngag dbang bstan dar criticized the view of Tsong kha pa and his followers by pointing out a few cases where their general rule fails.[20] Kuiji, however, argued there is no necessary connection between the subject being an empty term and the predicate being positive or negative—either implicative or non-implicative. Instead, he used a principle of propositional attitude to identify empty subject terms.[21]

6.5 The Principle of Propositional Attitude

At this point, it should be emphasized that, unlike Western formal logic, Buddhist and Indian logic was both a product and a means of the debating practice among various religious and philosophical groups in ancient India. The issue of empty subject terms is also closely connected with such practice. Primordial matter, which we discussed earlier, is considered an empty term by Buddhists. For the Sāṅkhyas, however, it is the most real thing. The criterion, then, for determining an empty term is not robust realism, pan-fictionalism, or conceptualism; rather, it rests on the doctrinal views of the specific parties involved in the debate.

Although the differences between various philosophical views may be apprehended through logical debates, these debates are in turn restricted by the respective philosophical positions of the specific disputants. For those who hold different or even contrary philosophical views, it is almost impossible to agree on whether a certain subject term, especially a metaphysical concept, is an empty term or not. But the empty subject terms discussed by Buddhists in most cases are just such metaphysical concepts—"self," "primordial matter," and "intrinsic nature." Some terms, for example, "sound" (*śabda*), may seem more real. But the Mīmāṃsakas regard sound to be permanent, while the Buddhists take it to be impermanent. Because of their different views, the term "sound" could be treated as a metaphysical concept and also become an empty term for one party in certain contexts.

Since empty terms are almost everywhere and they can change their status from time to time, we seem to be in a hopeless situation. But it is precisely in this situation that the key to the problem lies, namely, we have to acknowledge them. Acknowledging empty terms does not entail multiplying entities as Meinong or the Sarvāstivādins did; rather, it means to acknowledge the advocator of the subject term under discussion. For instance, when the Sāṅkhyas state a positive existential proposition with regard to primordial matter, it runs like this: "The primordial matter *that we accept* exists, because we see that the various individuals possess a similar general characteristic." When Buddhists state the negative existential proposition of the same subject, it should be: "The primordial matter *that you believe in* does not exist, because it cannot be apprehended."

This method is called the presuppositional distinguisher (*jianbie* 簡別) among the Chinese Buddhist logicians.[22] Its purpose is to distinguish between a statement that establishes one's own view and one that refutes the view of others. Self-establishing statements are indicated by phrases such as "we accept," "we admit," "we," and "as we said"; while the other-refuting statements are marked by phrases such as "you accept," "you believe," "you," and "holding." Statements that follow the rule of common establishment (*ubhayasiddhatva*), which states that the subject of an inferential statement (*pakṣa/dharmin*) must be established for both the proponent and the opponent in a debate, are called common inferences (*gong biliang* 共比量), and these are indicated by phrases like "commonly admitted."

In many cases, these presuppositional distinguishers apply to the subject (*dharmin*) of the proposition rather than the entire proposition, for example, "The primordial matter *that you believe in* does not exist." They seem to fall in between the two types of intentional operators identified by Priest (2016: 6–8). According to Priest, intentional verbs with non-phrase complements are called "intentional predicates," for instance, "I believe in primordial matter." Intentional verbs with sentential complements are called "intentional operators," for instance, "I believe that primordial matter is the first cause." But in our case, the proposition cannot be rephrased into "You believe in primordial matter" or "You believe that primordial matter does not exist." To a certain extent, this makes the issue more complicated, because it not only involves the truth or falsity, the meaningfulness or meaninglessness, of the propositions themselves, but also the intentional state of their advocators. And it involves not only one party, but at least two parties. Therefore, we call this approach the principle of propositional attitude.

Certainly, dealing with the propositional attitude requires more advanced logical techniques, such as epistemic logic and so forth. But in the debate practice of Buddhist logic, this propositional attitude can indicate clearly the advocator of the thesis under discussion, and, more importantly, whether the subject term is empty so as to avoid an unnecessary fallacy. With regard to the proposition considered here, "primordial matter does not exist," Shentai, in addition to using the method of paraphrase demonstrated in S2, offers us a way to deal with the problem by means of propositional attitude as follows:

(S3) Thesis: The primordial matter *that you believe in* does not exist.
Reason: Because there is non-apprehension of it.
Example: Just like a rabbit's horn.[23]

As compared to Dignāga's original statement "primordial matter does not exist, because there is non-apprehension of it," S3 emends the example "just like a rabbit's horn," and the phrase "that you believe in," indicating the propositional attitude. As a result, primordial matter as "you (i.e., Sāṅkhyas) believe in" is not an empty term at all for the Sāṅkhyas and there is no problem of empty subject terms. Their opponents, the Buddhists, can also talk about "the primordial matter that you believe in" as an indirect quotation from the Sāṅkhyas without worrying about difficulties introduced by empty terms. But for Buddhists this type of statement can only be used to refute their opponents, not to establish their own positions.

The principle of propositional attitude was widely used among Chinese Buddhist logicians. In Kuiji's works, many inferences are marked with phrases such as "we accept" and "you believe." In his theory of fallacy, each fallacy is further classified into those associated with self-establishing, other-refuting, and commonly agreed inferences. Exact parallels to this cannot be found in the logical theory of Indian and Tibetan Buddhism. But we do know that Dignāga attempted to develop the concept of own-subject (*svadharmin*) in his later work, *Pramāṇasamuccaya* III.2, and that Dharmakīrti further contrasted it with the concept of unrelated subject (*kevaladharmin*) in his *Pramāṇavārttika* IV.136–48. Two concepts seem to smuggle in an "attitude" component, even though such components are not explicitly identified. According to Tillemans, the unrelated subject "assures that the refutation presents the subject as the opponent conceives it, while the latter [i.e., *svadharmin*] is the proponent's actual subject that will serve as the basis upon which will be assessed the three characteristics of the logical reason" (1999: 281, n.32). Thus, these two concepts might have led to something like the principle of propositional attitude. The Chinese Buddhist logicians were explicitly marking these attitude components with presuppositional distinguishers. But in Indian and Tibetan Buddhism, developments along the lines of propositional attitude were overshadowed by conceptual subjects. Hence, the unrelated subject was understood more in the sense of a nominal subject, and there was a tendency to combine the notions of own-subject and conceptual subjects.[24] In other words, even the proponent's own intended subject is taken to be a conceptual thought rather than an entity accepted as real to the proponent himself. As a result, the distinction between the propositional attitude of a proponent and that of an opponent did not play an important role in dealing with the problem of empty subject terms.

On the Chinese side, Kuiji may have learned this method from his master Xuanzang. According to Kuiji's records, Xuanzang's most important academic achievement in India was emending the "Mahāyāna" inference of his teacher Jayasena and establishing his own "mind-only" inference. Both inferences are marked with the phrase "we accept" to indicate the propositional attitude of their proponents.[25] This principle of propositional attitude may have been a method popularly used by scholars at Nālandā University in the seventh century, or even earlier, since we have scattered sources that suggest Dharmapāla was familiar with this method.[26]

While the principle of propositional attitude solves the problem of empty subject terms, it raises a new issue: that is, the incommensurability between different parties involved in the debate. The mainstream Western logical system presupposes commensurability between rival parties by basing itself in a commonsense realism. But as a matter of fact, saying " 'sound is impermanent' is true because sound is impermanent" is no more convincing than saying " 'sound is permanent' is true because I believe sound is permanent." In a certain sense, the propositional attitude here is more privileged than the so-called objective facts in determining the truth or falsity of a given proposition. It is especially so when the matter under discussion is a metaphysical concept or a philosophical view. The danger of relying on the principle of propositional attitude lies in becoming trapped in the incommensurability of rival parties. Buddhist logicians were concerned with communication and commensurability between different parties involved in the debate from the very beginning, and they should be able to offer insights on the issue of incommensurability, but that must be the topic for another study.

To conclude, the problem of empty terms, like many other age-old philosophical problems, may never be definitively solved. This certainly has to do with the imperfection of logical systems. Besides Russell's theory of descriptions, introduced earlier, other alternative methods have been developed to tackle the problem. These include free logic, the logic of fiction, and the theory of possible worlds. The techniques that the Buddhist logicians adopted, especially the distinction between two types of negation and the principle of propositional attitude, may provide their Western colleagues with even more options.

More importantly, the variety of Buddhist approaches to the problem enriches our understanding of the philosophical issues regarding empty terms.

We realize that the so-called empty terms emerge from a more fundamental ontological commitment, and so the most effective approach must be to adopt an entirely new ontological position. This might be why the principle of conceptual subjects was dominant in late Indian and Tibetan Buddhism, while the Meinongian approach continues to be an active branch in analytic philosophy.[27]

7

Negative Judgments

Dharmakīrti's theory of negative judgments grew out of extensive discussions and debates on the cognition of nonexistent objects among various Buddhist and Indian philosophical schools. As is well known, a similar debate on the objectless presentations (*gegenstandslose Vorstellungen*) happened in the early development of phenomenology and analytic philosophy. Among various opinions on this controversial issue, I find that Dharmakīrti and Husserl hold similar views. Both of them have less interest in redefining the ontological status of nonexistent objects than Russell and Meinong. Rather, they engage themselves in analyzing the experiential structure of negative cognition and come up with a similar conclusion that negative judgments presuppose affirmative perceptions. This chapter will enrich our understanding of both thinkers.

7.1 How is a Negative Judgment Possible?

Consider the following statement:

> (A1) I walk into Alan's office, and see that Alan is not there. Then I realize that he is not in and say, "Alan is not in his office."

This might be a common experience we have in everyday life. In the following, I attempt to account for this experience philosophically. With this attempt,

I hope to come closer to the understanding of our very experience, which is the "*Sachen selbst*" that most scholars of phenomenology turn away from by involving themselves heavily in exegesis.

To begin with, let me introduce some controversies in the accounting for this phenomenon in the history of Indian and Buddhist philosophy. As compared to the Western philosophical tradition, Indian and Buddhist philosophy is more "negative" and treats issues such as negation, absence, and nonbeing more extensively, thereby providing us rich sources for the understanding of the experience of negative judgments.

First of all, some Naiyāyikas, for instance, Uddyotakara (Matilal 1968: 99; Guha 2013: 114–16) would argue that the very notion of "negative judgment" is self-contradictory, for they believe that negation is something that happens before judgment. It belongs to the realm of perception (*pratyakṣa*), so they would simplify A1 as follows:

(B1) I walk into Alan's office, and *see* that Alan is not there.

Here the word "see" is understood literally in the sense of perceiving with bare eyes, not in a loose sense of understanding or realizing. Seeing or perceiving is always a positive act on something. This way negation is brought into the realm of perception. Using Searle's (1969: 32–3) distinction between propositional and illocutionary negations, we can say that the Naiyāyikas restrict themselves to propositional negation $F(\sim p)$, a position shared by the mainstream Western philosophical tradition. For the Naiyāyikas, negation turns out to be an affirmation of negative facts. The very nature of affirmation ensures that negation is part of perception.

However, as perception is always of something, the validity of a perception relies heavily on the ontological status of its objects. Truly existent objects guarantee valid perception, while false or even nonexistent objects would surely lead to false perceptions. The perception of a double moon is false because the second moon does not really exist. The Naiyāyikas face the problem of how one can perceive a thing that does not exist. Reexamining B1, we will realize that it is actually impossible for me to say, "I see that Alan is *not* there." Instead, I may say, "I see the desk, chairs, or books in his office," and add:

(B2) I walk into Alan's office, and see Alan's *absence*.

This expression makes Alan's absence the object of perception; absence becomes something. This surprising step was actually what the Naiyāyikas were forced to take. Otherwise they would not succeed in reducing negation to perception. But this unique position that reifies absence or nonbeing was challenged by many other Indian philosophical schools, which brought the Naiyāyika theory of negation into a difficult situation.

Another approach to the issue is seen in two thinkers: the Buddhist Īśvarasena and the Mīmāṃsaka Kumārila. Instead of focusing on propositional negation, both of these thinkers switch their attention to the illocutionary aspect. On their view, A1 should be revised as:

(C1) I walk into Alan's office, and *do not see* that Alan is there.

The expression "do not see" (*adarśana*) is further defined with the technical term of non-cognition (*abhāva*). Non-cognition, in turn, is defined as the non-arising of cognitive acts, including perception, judgment, or inference. These two thinkers would also view the expression "negative judgment" as self-contradictory because non-cognition can be better characterized with the Searlian term "illocutionary negation," *~F (p)*. This illocutionary negation does not have to presuppose propositional negation. Negation is not really involved in the object side as I can either express C1 or say,

(C2) I walk into Alan's office, and do not see Alan.

The propositional negation, that is, the nonexistence of Alan, however, is built upon the illocutionary negation, that is, the non-cognition of Alan. It is through the very means of non-cognition that one learns about the negative facts such as "Alan is not there." Therefore, both Īśvarasena and Kumārila firmly insist that non-cognition is a separate means of knowledge (*pramāṇa*) over and above perception and inference (plus verbal testimony, analogy, and presumption in the case of the latter) (see Chapter 5 for further discussions). However, both of them have difficulty in explaining clearly what is the state of mind when neither perception nor inference is arising, which leads us to the third approach.

The third approach is found in the Buddhist philosopher Dharmakīrti, who developed his elaborate theory of negative judgments by arguing against the Naiyāyikas, his teacher Īśvarasena, and his elder contemporary Kumārila. For our purpose, it is sufficient to summarize some of his key points on the basis of Chapter 5 and further studies of Kellner (2001, 2003) and Watanabe (2002). First of all, he does not agree with the Naiyāyikas in reducing non-cognition to perception, nor with Īśvarasena and Kumārila in counting non-cognition as an independent means of knowledge. As we discussed earlier, the former view only accounts for propositional negation while the latter only explains illocutionary negation. Instead, he includes non-cognition (*anupalabdhi*) under inference and treats it as one of the three evidences (*hetu*) that ensure sound inferences. Therefore, he would take "negative judgment" to mean literally that "Negation is judgment."

Second, to make non-cognition a valid inference, Dharmakīrti distinguishes between non-cognitions of perceptible and "imperceptible objects." Imperceptible objects refer to supersensory or abstract objects, the non-cognition of which, according to him, cannot determine their existence. For instance, from the non-cognition of ghosts one cannot conclude that ghosts do not exist. On the contrary, the absence of perceptible objects is proved if and only if they are not perceived when all the conditions for perception are fulfilled. Dharmakīrti limits himself to the discussion of the non-cognition of these perceptible objects, and only deals with negation of empirical objects or facts. As we will see later, this position has its advantages in avoiding issues involved with negative existential propositions.

Third, the non-cognition of perceptible objects, being an inference, is based on affirmative perceptions. According to Dharmakīrti, we have to know that there is nothing there through inference instead of simply through seeing or hearing. The fact that "there is *no* pottery on the table" is known through an inferential judgment that is based on the perception of the table instead of the pottery. In other words, the negation of the existence of pottery is an inferential judgment based on the normal perceptions of things other than pottery, for example, the table and so on.

Applying these points to the case discussed earlier, we have the following formula:

> (D1) I walk into Alan's office, and see only the desk, chairs, and books. Then I realize that he is not in and say, "Alan is not in his office."

The first sentence indicates affirmative perceptions of things other than Alan. On the basis of these perceptions, I come up with an inference as expressed in the second sentence. As all the objects under discussion are perceptible, this statement would reflect Dharmakīrti's view on the issue fairly well.

7.2 Negation is Secondary

Now how would Husserl address this controversial issue? Husserl's view on negative judgments can be found in his later work *Experience and Judgment*, where a separate section is devoted to negation. A more extensive treatment, believed to be an earlier unabridged version of this section, is included in the *Analyses Concerning Passive and Active Synthesis*. Some scattered sources can also be found in his *Logical Investigations*, especially sections 11, 30–35 of Investigation Six.

As compared to his elaborations on other topics, these minor sections are far from enough to build a phenomenological theory of negative judgments. Therefore, it is not surprising to find that very few secondary sources deal with Husserl's view on negation. Even when there are a few, such as of Harvey and Hintikka (1991), Krysztofiak (1992), and Benoist (2001), most of them were inspired by relevant discussions in analytic philosophy. It is understandable that most of the contemporary discussions on this issue are found in analytic philosophy, especially in the field of philosophical logic. These technical discussions deal exclusively with propositional negation and make no attempt to explore the experiential basis of negation. In this connection, Husserl's brief but brilliant analysis of "the origin of negation" contributed to our understanding of the experiential aspect of this logical issue, which is exactly where I look for inspiration in Indian and Buddhist philosophy.

However, it is wrong to claim that Husserl has moved away from the mainstream conception of propositional negation. It is true that he has attempted to extend negation to the subpropositional level, and explored a conception of negation as a cognitive act instead of negation as belonging to the meaning itself. In other words, he demonstrated an illocutionary view of negation. However, as is convincingly argued by Benoist (2001), he eventually chooses a propositional view of negation. This reveals the ambiguity of the phenomenological theory of negation, "standing between act and meaning, and between language and perception" (21). Before carefully examining Husserl's view on the issue, it can be anticipated that with this ambiguity or hesitation between an illocutionary and a propositional view of negation Husserl has come very close to the position of Dharmakīrti, who also maintains a middle way between the propositional view of the Naiyāyikas and the illocutionary view of Īśvarasena and Kumārila.

In his analysis of negation, Husserl (1973: 90) asserts firmly that "negation is not first the business of the act of predicative judgment but that in its original form it already appears in the prepredicative sphere of receptive experience."

He demonstrates this view by engaging himself in the phenomenological description of the origin of negation in prepredicative experience, using the famous example of perceiving a red ball. In such an experience, if we observe a ball with uniformly red color continuously, either by standing in front of it and going around or rotating it, then our intention of anticipation is fulfilled: "it is a red ball." If, however, in the progress of the perception, the back side is revealed to be "not red, but green," "not spherical, but dented," then the original anticipation that ran "uniformly red, uniformly spherical" is disappointed. Thereupon, we have the negative judgments: "it is not entirely red"; "it is not perfectly spherical."

As we will see below, Husserl's example can be compared to the case of walking into Alan's office, which we discussed earlier. Both cases indicate a prepredicative experience of negation. The Indian and Buddhist philosophers would not dispute with Husserl on the possibility of such type of experience. The key, however, lies in the philosophical accounts of such experience, which is exactly the point of controversy in the Indian side.

Husserl draws two important conclusions from his previous analysis. First, negation presupposes "normal perception" (Husserl 1973: 91; 2001: 71). Here the "normal perception" refers to the perceptual process that proceeds without obstruction, as is seen in the earlier case when the red ball is perceived. Contemporary interpretations such as those of Harvey and Hintikka (1991: 61) and Krysztofiak (1992: 210) seem not to grasp this point and merge it with Husserl's second conclusion, which I will introduce later. To my understanding, this point rather indicates that negation is secondary as compared to the normal affirmative perception, and it is a modification of the latter. Husserl (1973: 292) explicitly states this point elsewhere: "The negative judgment is not a basic form." In his example, the negative judgments "it is not entirely red" or "it is not a perfect ball" are built upon the normal perceptions of greenness or dented shape of the back side. Without these subsequent perceptions, one cannot negate the original anticipation of redness or spherical shape.

If applying Husserl's phenomenological analysis to the current case, we will have a richer account of the experience, which reveals more details on the structure of a negative cognition:

(H1) I walk into Alan's office, and see only the desk, chairs, and books. Then I realize that he is not in and say, "Alan is not in his office."

The same as in D1, here the affirmative statement "[I] see only the desk, chairs, and books" substitutes for the negative ones "[I] see that Alan is not there" or "[I] do not see that Alan is there." The normal unobstructed perceptions of desk or chairs indicate what is going on at the perceptual level when I walk into Alan's office. Definitely, I do not *perceive* that Alan is not there; rather, I see actual things such as the desk and books.

This implies that Husserl does not have to follow the Naiyāyikas to admit to the ontological status of negative facts as a consequence of extending negation to the perceptual level. However, these affirmative perceptions of the desk and so on also eliminate the possibility of speculating about non-cognition as an independent means of knowledge, as in the case of Īśvarasena and Kumārila. On Husserl's view, a careful analysis of the cognitive process on the perceptual or intellectual level can account for the knowledge of negative facts. There is no need to introduce a mysterious state of non-cognition. As we see, this is exactly the strategy that Dharmakīrti takes to approach the issue. He argues against the Naiyāyikas, Īśvarasena, and Kumārila, refuting their extreme propositional or illocutionary views of negation. While reducing negative cognition to inference, he still emphasizes that negative judgments are formed on the basis of affirmative perceptions. So he would fully agree with H1.

But how does the affirmative perception lead to negative judgments? To understand this, we have to turn to Husserl's (1973: 91) second conclusion, where he further specifies that negation, as a modification of original normal perception, is realized "by the disappointment of protentional anticipations of belief" (see Husserl 2001: 71). This point was elaborated in various ways by Harvey and Hintikka (1991) and Krysztofiak (1992), and eventually overshadowed the first conclusion discussed earlier. I agree that this observation of Husserl demonstrates his most original contribution to the issue of negation. He might be the first Western philosopher who analyzes negative judgments in terms of its temporal dimension, as the key term "protention" indicates in the protention–primary impression–retention structure of time consciousness. Negation presupposes not only normal perceptions, but also anticipations and beliefs, which are important components in the protentional dimension of consciousness. For Husserl, every cognition starts with protention, which is in the very nature of intentionality. The actual cognitive process consists in the fulfillment of such protentional anticipation. In his own example, the belief in "uniformly red, uniformly spherical" is the protentional anticipation. Its fulfillment is realized by a modification of disappointment: "not entirely red, but partly green," "not spherical, but dented." Therefore, with the disappointment of protentional anticipations, one comes up with the negative judgments: "it is not entirely red"; "it is not perfectly a ball."

Applying the second conclusion to our case, we will have to reformulate the statement in the following way:

> (H2) I walk into Alan's office, expecting and believing he is in, but see only the desk, chairs, and books. Then I realize that he is not in and say, "Alan is not in his office."

To interpolate the phrase "expecting and believing he is in" is a crucial step in applying the phenomenological analysis to the current case. Without this anticipation, the perceptions of the desk or books do not really fit the context, for these objects are not the subject of concern at all. Only in contrast to the anticipation of Alan do these perceptions start to make sense in the way that they disappointed this anticipation.

So far, it seems that Husserl's accounts of negation are too "negative," as he characterizes it in terms of the "disappointment" of anticipation and lists it along with doubt and possibility as a "modification" of consciousness. This implies that negation turns out to be "obstruction" or "failure" of normal affirmative cognitions, which makes it an invalid or secondary act, as Husserl (1973: 292) explicitly states: "*The act of negation of the ego consists in the exclusion of validity*, and the *secondary intentional character* [of negation] is already implicit in this expression" (emphasis in the original). This may confirm the mainstream view on the epistemological role of negation or negative judgments in Western philosophy, but does not harmonize with the positive role that negation or non-cognition plays in the epistemological systems of Indian and Buddhist philosophy. Although the Naiyāyikas, Mīmāṃsakas, and Buddhists were debating about the way that negation takes place, they did not doubt its important role in their theories of knowledge. They all distinguish negation from the "modifications" of cognition that include erroneous cognition, desire, and memory, which are called pseudo-perception (*pratyaksābhāsa*), and consider it a valid means of knowledge, either in the form of perception, inference, or independently as non-cognition.

Despite those "negative" characteristics attributed to negation, does it play a positive role in Husserl's phenomenology? We do not see an explicit answer to the question in his own writings. Instead, it is found in some contemporary interpretations. One answer is given by Lohmar (1992: 188), who understands "negation as categorial intuition." Offering no direct reference from Husserl to support his interpretation, Lohmar nevertheless is justified to make such a move. As the act that disappoints protentional anticipations, negation certainly belongs to the phase of intentional fulfillment. Categorial intuition, however, plays an important role in fulfilling intentions. Lohmar (1992: 189) explains the relationship between negation and categorial intuition in Husserl's example of the red ball in the following way:

> Der Akt der Negation beginnt, als ob die erwartete eigenschaftliche Bestimmung "rot" prädikativ konstituiert werden sollte. Der erforderliche Akt kategorialer Anschauung kann sich aber nicht mehr auf anschaulich

> erfüllte Sonderintentionen aufbauen. Er muß bereits auf Surrogate aus Erinnerungen und evtl. aus der frischen Retention zurückgreifen. Hierbei zeigt sich die Funktion der induktiven Gewißheiten für die Motivation der Sonderwahrnehmung erfaßt werden, sondern das vorprädikativ bereits fraglich gewordene rot.

Here, it is important to note that the categorial intuition required for the act of negation does not build itself upon "the intuitively fulfilled particular intentions." Instead, it has to fall back on memory or fresh retention so as to fulfill the original anticipation of the red. Therefore, the subject that is concerned in the negative judgment is not the green color that is actually perceived, but still the red, which demonstrates the function of inductive certainty (*induktiven Gewißheiten*). The categorial intuition that works closely with memory or retention is certainly not sensory intuition, the once-for-all grasping of sensory objects. In Husserl's terminology, categorial intuition rather refers to the acts of synthesis or abstraction that may be completed in more than one step. Therefore, he would not agree with the Naiyāyikas who reduce negation to perception, which is closely linked to sensory intuition, but rather agrees with Dharmakīrti's view that reduces negation to inference, which is in general of an inductive nature in the Buddhist logical system.

Another answer is given by Harvey and Hintikka (1991) and Krysztofiak (1992), who understand negation as "modality" or "creation of possible worlds." Being inspired by relevant discussions in analytic philosophy, these interpretations are not necessarily faithful to Husserl himself. For instance, Krysztofiak attempted to deal with the so-called existential negative propositions (e.g., "Pegasus does not exist") and proposed his theory of the "creation of possible worlds" as a solution to this paradox, along with some other famous proposals: description theory, free logic, logic of fiction, and so on. To my knowledge, however, Husserl himself was not so much concerned with such existential negative propositions, although he lived through the period when this problem was discussed and debated. It would be interesting to examine carefully how he would address this puzzling issue, given his close relationship with the Brentanian and Meinongian traditions. Probably, he would agree with Dharmakīrti again in distinguishing between the negation of perceptible things (e.g., "It is not a red ball") and the negation of imperceptible things (e.g., "Ghosts do not exist"). The latter type of negation is linked to the paradox of negative existential propositions, but Dharmakīrti admits that his theory of non-cognition is not able to deal with this type of negation.

As far as empirical perceptible objects are concerned, however, the theories as developed by Husserl and Dharmakīrti are powerful enough to explain the negative judgment regarding such objects. By way of conclusion, let me highlight the main points that are shared by both thinkers:

1. Both of them focus on the negation of empirical objects and show little interest in examining the ontological issues involved with the object side.
2. They both hold that negative judgments presuppose and build themselves upon affirmative perceptions, and hence are secondary in relation to the latter.
3. They both carry out detailed analysis of the experiential structure of negative cognition. Husserl further reveals its protentional dimension. Negation is therefore understood as motivated by disappointment of protentional anticipations.
4. They both take a middle-way position between the propositional and illocutionary views of negation, which makes their theories outstanding in their own tradition.

Despite all these striking similarities, however, it is important to be reminded that their theories of negative judgments were developed in very different traditions. It is very hard to draw direct correspondence between their respective theoretical framework and relevant concepts involved. I hope that my attempt will not turn out to be a failure, being negated by scholars from both traditions.

8

Typology of Nothing

Parmenides expelled nonbeing from the realm of knowledge and forbade us to think or talk about it. But still there has been a long tradition of naysayings throughout the history of Western and Eastern philosophy. Are those philosophers talking about the same nonbeing or nothing? If not, how do their concepts of nothing differ from each other? Could there be different types of nothing?

Leibniz once famously argued against the possibility of there being more than one void. He maintains that if there could be more than one void, then there could be two voids of exactly the same shape and size. These two voids would be perfect twins (Sorensen 2017: sec. 9). Leibniz's argument suggests that if we are dealing with empty space, then a type of nothing potentially has "shape" or "size." But the variety of traditional conceptions of nothing is much more complicated than this.

Surveying the traditional classifications of nothing or nonbeing in the East and West have led me to develop a typology of nothing that consists of three main types: (1) privative nothing, commonly known as absence; (2) negative nothing, the altogether not or absolute nothing; and finally (3) original nothing, the nothing that is equivalent to being. I do not claim that these exhaust the types of nothing in which many other philosophers had more finely grained classification schemes. For instance, the Neo-Platonist Ammonios Hermeiou and the Indian Yogācāras distinguished five different types of nothing, whereas Marius Victorinus (another Neo-Platonist), Immanuel Kant, and mainstream Indian philosophy had developed various fourfold schemes. However, I think my typology will suffice for my purpose which is to examine the similarities and differences between the conceptions of nothing in Heidegger, Daoism, and Buddhism. The reason why I choose these three philosophical strains to test my typology of nothing is not only because I am familiar with them, but also because they each respectively represent the developing concepts of nothing in the West, China, and India.

The logical positivist Rudolf Carnap once criticized the Western tradition of metaphysics by taking Heidegger's theory of nothing as an extreme case of meaningless discourse (1931: 233). Similarly, in the eyes of orthodox Confucian and Hindu scholars, both Daoism and Buddhism were seen as passive, negative, and even destructive to intellectual and social norms. In fact, these scholars condemned them as heresies and were determined to eliminate their influence on Chinese and Indian minds. It is no accident that their opponents developed a "negative" impression of these traditions. These are three of the very few philosophical strains that have launched themselves into the wonderland of negativity by developing respectively the concepts of nothing (*Nichts*), nothing (*wu* 無), and emptiness (*śūnyatā*).

8.1 Original Nothing

In his major work *Being and Time*, Heidegger apparently did not treat nothing as a central issue. Only in his analysis of *Angst*, one of the fundamental attunements (*Befindlichkeit*) of Dasein, does he touch upon this concept. The idea of *Angst* is deeply rooted in the Judeo-Christian tradition. In a long footnote in section 40 on "The fundamental attunement of *Angst* as an eminent disclosedness of *Da-sein*," Heidegger refers to Augustine, Luther, and

Kierkegaard to support his distinction between *Angst* and fear (*Furcht*). With regard to *Angst*, Heidegger says:

> The fact that what is threatening is *nowhere* characterizes what *Angst* is about. *Angst* "does not know" what it is about which it is anxious. But "nowhere" does not mean nothing; rather, region in general lies therein, and disclosedness of the world in general for essentially spatial being-in. Therefore, what is threatening cannot approach from a definite direction within nearness, it is already "there"—and yet nowhere. It is so near that it is oppressive and stifles one's breath—and yet it is nowhere. In what *Angst* is about, the "it is nothing and nowhere" becomes manifest. (Heidegger 1963: 186; Stambaugh 1996: 174–5; emphases in the original)

It is nothing (*Nichts*) and nowhere (*nirgends*), and yet the disclosedness of the world lies within it. This reminds us of God being depicted in negative terms within the mystical Christian tradition. In contrast to the philosophical discussions of nothing, as found in early Western philosophers, such as Parmenides and Plato, the Christian mystics who developed the negative theology regard nothing as an experience. Their view has influenced many classical German philosophers, including Schelling and Hegel. In this sense, nothing is not an abstract concept, but rather a reality that can be experienced. This is similar to the Eastern mystical tradition of Daoism that emphasizes the sagely practice of experiencing nothing (*shengren ti wu* 聖人體無).

Of course, it is not so easy to experience nothing. In fact, Heidegger admits that such an experience is rare. In Heidegger's *What Is Metaphysics*, he states: "Does such an attunement, in which man is brought before the nothing itself, occur in human *Dasein*? It can and does occur, although rarely enough and only for a moment, in the fundamental mood of *Angst*" (1978: 111; 1998: 88, with my modification). In this work of 1929, we find the most extensive discussion of nothing by Heidegger. Most of the work illustrates how nothing is revealed and experienced in *Angst*. Moreover, he develops another theme that is not seen in *Being and Time*, which is the relationship between being and nothing. He says, "Nothing does not remain the indeterminate opposite of beings but unveils itself as belonging to the being of beings" (Heidegger 1978: 120; 1998: 94). Furthermore, he states that "in the being of beings the nihilation (*Nichten*) of nothing occurs" (Heidegger 1978: 115; 1998: 91). We can infer from these statements that Heidegger takes nothing to be equivalent to being.

The idea that nothing and being are equivalent can be found in many of Heidegger's works. For instance, "Being: Nothing: Same . . . Nothing is the characteristic (*Kennzeichnung*) of Being."[1] Reinhard May, who studied these expressions, tries to prove their connection with relevant statements that are found in Daoism and Chan Buddhism. These statements include: "Being and nothing giving rise to each other" (*Dao-De-Jing* Ch. 2); "The things of the world arise from being. And being arises from nothing" (*Dao-De-Jing* Ch. 40); "Being is none other than nothing, nothing is none other than being" (*Xin-Xin-Ming* 信心銘, T2010: 377a6–7). May (1996: 26–8) maintains that all of these Daoist and Chan Buddhist writings were already translated into German in or before the 1920s, and so Heidegger may have read these sources and become influenced by them.

Heidegger, however, only admits Hegel's contribution on this point. He cites a statement from Hegel's *Science of Logic*: "Pure being and pure nothing are the same." Pure being and pure nothing are two concepts in the beginning of Hegel's logical system. They are the same because they are indeterminate, immediate, and pure. But Heidegger disagrees with Hegel on how and why they are the same. He says: "Being and nothing do belong together, not because both—from the point of view of the Hegelian concept of thought—agree in their indeterminateness and immediacy, but rather because being itself is essentially finite and manifests itself only in the transcendence of a *Dasein* that is held out into nothing" (Heidegger 1978: 120; 1998: 94–5). Here, "the transcendence of Dasein" is discussed earlier in the same work: "Being held out into nothing—as *Dasein* is—on the ground of concealed *Angst* is its surpassing of beings as a whole. It is transcendence" (Heidegger 1978: 118; 1998: 93). *Dasein* transcends the totality of beings and therefore reaches the being itself. Meanwhile, *Dasein* is also "held out" into nothing, therefore being and nothing become identical in the experiential dimension of *Dasein*.

Another theme that Heidegger devoted himself to is the relationship between nothing and negativity, a concept again bearing a Hegelian mark. In Hegel's system, negativity is apparently more active and important than pure nothing. It is the engine of the Hegelian dialectics and makes becoming, movement, and development possible through its force of *Aufhebung*. Although Heidegger (1978: 117; 1998: 86) insists that "nothing is the origin of negation, not vice versa," he closely follows Hegel when he describes how nothing functions through negation and refusal. We can see this in two of Heidegger's works that were written in the 1930s but only recently published.

> Fullness is pregnant with the originary "not"; making full is not *yet* and *no longer* gifting, both in *counter-resonance*, refused in the very hesitating, and thus the *charming-moving-unto* in the removal-unto in the removal-unto. Here [is] above all the swaying not-character of be-ing as enowning. (Heidegger 1999: 189; emphases in the original)

> The questioning of the history of being not only experiences nothing not as void (*Nichtiges*), when this questioning requests the being itself in the fullness of its essential swaying, nothing is experienced as enownment (*Er-eignung*). (Heidegger 1997: 313; my translation)

Here enowning (*Ereignis*) or enownment (*Ereignung*) functions as the provider or giver of being and time, and it is the "it" in the phrase "it gives/there is" (*es gibt*). Meanwhile, Heidegger stresses that the withdrawal or refusal that is not providing or giving also belongs essentially to the enowning itself. It is this withdrawal or refusal that makes providing or giving possible. Therefore, in the withdrawal or refusal that is located in the heart of enowning, we see an original nothing, which is the ultimate ground for negation and negativity.

The term "original nothing" (*nihil originarium*) appears in Heidegger's writings only a few times. For instance, when discussing the world as nothing, he says: "The world is the nothing that originally temporalizes itself and simply arises in and with the temporalizing (*Zeitigung*). We, therefore, call the world the original nothing (*nihil originarium*)."[2] Nevertheless, this term captures very well the basic meaning of nothing in Heidegger's usage, namely, as something experienced by *Dasein*'s *Angst*, equivalent to being, and functioning through negation and withdrawal.

By using "original nothing," Heidegger also distances himself from other types of nothing that were discussed by previous philosophers. It is generally agreed that what Parmenides forbade us to talk about is "the altogether not" (τό μηδαμῆ μηδαμῶς ὄν). Since Plato, philosophers have tried to break this curse, but they were only approaching an "absence." In Kant's fourfold classification of nothing, these two senses of nothing are respectively called negative nothing (*nihil negativum*) and privative nothing (*nihil privativum*). He characterizes the former as "the empty object without concept" that is the impossible, for example, a two-sided rectilinear figure, and the latter as "the empty object of a concept," for example, a shadow or cold.[3] For many philosophers, these are the two basic types of nothing. I therefore take them to be the first two types in my classification scheme. But Heidegger's sense of original nothing seems to have nothing to do with them. Instead, this nothing signifies alternatively to his key concept of being. Nothing as being is also one of the four types of nothing for the Neo-Platonist Marius Victorinus.[4] Its traces can be found in many classical German thinkers such as F. H. Jacobi, J. G. Hamann, Schelling, Hegel, and F. von Baader. So, I include original nothing as the third type of nothing in my classification scheme. With these three types of nothing in mind, we can now discuss the Daoist concept of nothing.

8.2 Nothing

In early Daoism, nothing may not have been a central concept as "*Dao*," but even at this stage it is an essential aspect of *Dao*. Its position was further elevated with the development of the Xuan School. The Neo-Confucian scholars, also known as "*Dao*-scholars," were not necessarily upset by the idea of *Dao*, but often reacted strongly against nothing. Nothing may not be the central concept of Daoist philosophy, but it is surely the most characteristic Daoist concept.

According to Pang (1999: 348–63), the concept of nothing as discussed in the rich canons of Chinese philosophy can be classified as having three different types. These include "nothing as absence," "absolute nothing," and "nothing as being," which are signified, respectively, by the characters *wang* (亡), *wu* (无), and *wu* (無). Interestingly, these three types correspond to the three major types of nothing that I identified among Western philosophers, namely, privative nothing (*nihil privativum*), negative nothing (*nihil negativum*), and original nothing (*nihil originarium*). It is now pertinent to consider what type of nothing the Daoists were talking about.

Many contemporary scholars distinguish two senses of nothing in Lao Zi's *Dao-De-Jing*.[5] One is the empirical or commonsense usage referring to empty space. This usage is found especially in chapter 11 of the *Dao-De-Jing*, where nothing functions inside the hub, a pot, and the dwelling. The other is nothing in its metaphysical sense, referring to the source or origin of all existents, and found in key passages of the *Dao-De-Jing*, for example, chapters 2 and 40.[6] This distinction, however, becomes irrelevant if we attempt to match Daoist nothing to my typology of nothing. Both space and the origin of all existents are actual existence with real function. They are called nothing only because they are formless and imageless. So nothing for Lao Zi, either in its empirical or metaphysical sense, is the "nothing as being" or the original nothing.

In the *Dao-De-Jing*, there is also a large number of compounds in the form of "non-*x*" or "no-*x*," for example, nonaction (*wu-wei* 無爲) and no-name (*wu-ming* 無名), where the word *wu* (non-, no-) functions as a prefix in the compound and cannot act independently as a noun or a philosophical concept. Its meaning is close to the privative nothing or nothing as absence. The Daoist classics never seem to mention the absolute or negative nothing, which usually indicates logical impossibility as in the case of late Moist classics.[7]

In any case, the concept of nothing as discussed in the Daoist philosophical context falls under the category of original nothing or nothing as being. It is elaborated in two aspects. The first is the cosmogonical or vertical dimension, with the emphasis of nothing being the source or origin of existents: "The things of the world arise from being. And being arises from nothing."[8] It is this ability of giving rise to all existents that makes nothing the true original nothing. The same idea is elaborated in the *Zhuang-Zi*: "The myriad things come forth from nonbeing (*wuyou* 無有). Being cannot bring being into being; it must come forth from nonbeing, and nonbeing is singularly nonbeing."[9] The Xuan School, represented by Wang Bi, further develops this line of thinking and interprets nothing as the "origin" (*ben* 本) of all things. In comparison to its Western counterparts, the Daoist nothing is more "original" by emphasizing its cosmogonical dimension.

The second is the ontological or horizontal dimension that emphasizes "being and nothing giving rise to each other."[10] The mutual arising of being and nothing horizontally illuminates the identity and transformation between pure being and pure nothing. The formless, imageless original nothing, through its identity with and transformation into being, establishes its ontological position in the sense of nothing as being. This runs parallel to the ontologies of Hegel and Heidegger.

Certain tension exists between the two dimensions, however, and many commentators have attempted to explain the apparent contradiction. In my view, the failure of classical Chinese philosophers, such as Lao Zi, to distinguish ontology from cosmology or cosmogony contributes to this tension. The admixture of cosmogonical and ontological approaches that dominates classical Chinese philosophy probably owes its existence to the centrality of *sheng* (生; begetting, generating, giving rise to) in Daoist and Confucian metaphysics. Exactly for the same reason, original nothing in Lao Zi and Daoist philosophy is realized in its more complete "original" form than in the works of Western philosophers such as Heidegger, who only stress its ontological dimension.

8.3 Emptiness

Let's turn to emptiness in Buddhist philosophy and its relationship to nothing. In early and sectarian Buddhism, the concept of emptiness was employed to interpret the foundational Buddhist doctrine of no-self. It became one of the key Buddhist concepts with the rise of Perfection of Wisdom literature and its interpretation by the Madhyamaka scholars. The orthodox Hindu scholars, who often classified Buddhist philosophy into four major schools, namely, Sarvāstivāda realism, Sautrāntika indirect realism, Yogācāra idealism, and Madhyamaka nihilism, were especially critical of the latter. In their view, emptiness may not have been the central concept of Buddhism, but it was no doubt the most characteristic of Buddhist philosophy.

In the history of Indian philosophy, different schemes were developed for classifying nothing or nonbeing (*abhāva*). The mainstream Vaiśeṣikas, Naiyāyikas, and Mīmāṃsakas classified nonbeing into four types, namely, prior nonbeing (*prāgabhāva*), posterior nonbeing (*dhvaṃsa*), mutual nonbeing (*anyonyābhāva*), and absolute nonbeing (*atyantābhāva*). These four types can be subsumed into two more basic types: absolute nonbeing and mutual nonbeing. The latter covers the first three of four types, which are its manifestations in temporal and spatial dimensions. Mutual nonbeing corresponds to privative nothing or absence in my typology, while absolute nonbeing is the negative nothing with respect to "the altogether not." This popular scheme, however, does not include emptiness. Among the Indic sources that I have encountered, only a Yogācāra Buddhist text adds emptiness to the scheme as the fifth type of nonbeing. It is called the "ultimate nonbeing" (*paramārthāsat*) and interpreted as "devoid of intrinsic nature" (*niḥsvabhāva*), which is exactly the definition of emptiness.[11]

It is generally agreed that the Perfection of Wisdom literature and its Madhyamaka interpretation, while aiming at criticizing and denying intrinsic nature, made emptiness a central Buddhist concept. Intrinsic nature (*svabhāva*) was a key concept in Abhidharma scholasticism, which characterized the unanalyzable elements (*dharma*) of all existents. In this understanding, the intrinsic nature of each and every element should be distinctive and consistent, otherwise their distinction will collapse. Meanwhile, their consistent, even permanent, nature does not imply that existents made of elements do not go through change or transformation. All the elements and existents, as long as they are conditioned, must dependently arise and cease.

In the Madhyamaka view, however, the concept of intrinsic nature is incompatible with the foundational Buddhist doctrine of dependent arising. Nāgārjuna argues, "The origination of intrinsic nature from causes and conditions is illogical, since intrinsic nature originated from causes and conditions would become contingent. How could there be contingent intrinsic nature? Intrinsic nature is not contingent, nor is it dependent on others."[12] By upholding the doctrine of dependent origination, one must give up and deny intrinsic nature, as Nāgārjuna declares: "Whatever is dependently originated, I claim it is emptiness."[13] He holds that all those in the net of causal arising—either conventional existence or its elements—are devoid of intrinsic nature and empty. For the Ābhidharmikas, such conventional existence—for instance, a desk or person—is conceptually constructed, and hence lack intrinsic nature, but their building blocks are those elements embedded within intrinsic nature. Nāgārjuna insists that even those building blocks, as long as they arise and cease in the causal network, are "conceptually constructed."[14]

There are at least two ways of understanding this claim of emptiness. If all existents are conceptually constructed, as with illusions and hallucinatory objects, then emptiness in this sense is absolute or negative nothing as in the case of the son of a barren woman or square-circle, both indicating logical impossibility. This will inevitably lead to a nihilist end that negates all existents, which, as a matter of fact, dominates classical and contemporary interpretations of the Madhyamaka tradition.[15] The other way, however, emphasizes that absolute reality such as *dharma*-nature (*dharmatā*) or thatness (*tattva*) is revealed through the idea of emptiness that denies intrinsic nature.[16] In this view, emptiness comes close to original nothing or nothing as being. Nāgārjuna himself seems unwilling to fall into either extreme when he claims that emptiness is "the middle way,"[17] which is beyond nonbeing and being. From the viewpoint of my typology of nothing, if emptiness is beyond negative nothing (the extreme of nonbeing) and original nothing (the extreme of being), then it would fall under privative nothing. This observation is supported by the very definition of emptiness as "devoid of intrinsic nature," which is a constant negation and antidote of any reification, even emptiness itself, and therefore "emptiness is empty."[18] But when emptiness is expanded to negate all existents at the ultimate level, it will cease to be a mutual nonbeing in the sense of absence and become an absolute negative nonbeing. The Mādhyamikas themselves may not admit this, but their theory inevitably leads to this end.

In the Yogācāra school, even though emptiness is not as central as it is in the Madhyamaka school, the Yogācāras understood it very differently. They refer to a passage from an early Buddhist text, *Cūḷasuññata-sutta*, which is never cited with approval by the Mādhyamikas in their extensive discussion on emptiness (Nagao 1991: 210). The text says: "One rightly observes that because something does not exist in a given place, [therefore] this [place] is empty of that [thing]. Moreover, one knows in accordance with reality that whatever remains in this place [apart from that thing] still exists, and it is something that exists in this place."[19] In this case, emptiness is understood in terms of privation or absence, or, in an Indian term, mutual nonbeing. This type of nonbeing is always relative to something existent. It is in this sense that emptiness serves as an antidote to intrinsic nature in Madhyamaka.

The Yogācāras understood emptiness in terms of its root meaning of absence and defined "the characteristic of emptiness as the nonexistence of the duality [of subject and object] and the existence of that nonexistence."[20] The duality of subject and object, in their epistemologically oriented project, is regarded as a conceptual construction on the basis of existent conscious processes. The concept of emptiness denies the existence of these conceptual constructions, yet asserts the existence of consciousness (*vijñāna*), thusness (*tathatā*), or dharma-realm (*dharmadhātu*). In this respect, emptiness is equivalent to the so-called wondrous being (*miao-you* 妙有) and therefore comes close to the original nothing or nothing as being in my typology of nothing.

Later Tibetan Buddhists characterized the Yogācāra way of understanding emptiness as "other-emptiness" (*gzhan stong*), in contrast to the "self-emptiness" (*rang stong*) held by the Mādhyamikas, and condemned the former way of understanding as heresy. This understanding of emptiness as wondrous being, however, became dominant in East Asian Buddhism, a development based on the influence of the Yogācāra as well as the Daoist sense of original nothing. As a result, Buddhist emptiness and Daoist nothing were easily confused.[21] Masao Abe (1985: 128–30), for instance, while discussing the superiority of negativity in Eastern philosophy, treated both Daoist nothing and Buddhist emptiness as equivalent to wondrous being. In his discussion, both are understood to be original nothing or nothing as being.

8.4 Why is there Something Rather than Nothing?

By studying the similarities and differences between the concept of nothing in Heidegger, Daoism, and Buddhism, I have tested my threefold typology of nothing. If we distinguish the conceptions of nothing into three basic types, namely, privative, negative, and original nothing, then Heidegger's and Daoism's conception of nothing can be characterized as "original nothing." The unique Daoist cosmogonical-ontological approach renders nothing more "original" than its parallels in Western philosophy. In contrast, the emptiness in Madhyamaka Buddhism is basically a type of privative nothing, but its tendency to negate all existents at the ultimate level leads to negative nothing. And finally, the emptiness in Yogācāra Buddhism is basically nothing as absence or privation, but its affirmation of ultimate reality leads to original nothing. The latter sense of emptiness was more influential among East Asian Buddhists, and more easily confused with the Daoists' original nothing.

With this analysis, I hope that I have clarified some confusion in the understanding of nothing in Heidegger, Daoism, and Buddhism. This typology of nothing also sheds light on the central philosophical issue of "what there is not." The perplexity of this issue is attributed to the fact that nonbeing or nothing, by its very nature, escapes from falling into a being or something and thus resists any attempt of definition or characterization. In the history of Western philosophy, the mystery of nothing is usually associated with two equally mysterious questions. One is why, according to Parmenides, cannot we think or talk about nonbeing? This question becomes even more intriguing in contrast to the fact that we can talk about nonbeing or nothing with ease in our ordinary language. The other is the famous Leibnizian–Heideggerian question: "Why is there something rather than nothing?" which has been taken to be the fundamental question of metaphysics.

According to my typology of nothing, when Parmenides forbade us from thinking or talking about nonbeing, he was warning us against the altogether not or absolute nothing, for example, square-circle and the son of a barren woman. It is evident that this type of nothing was mainly a logician's concern, including Moists, Hindu, and Buddhist logicians, and contemporary analytic philosophers. Given its nature of being logically contradictory and impossible, this type of nothing, as predicted by Parmenides, does not really enter into the realm of knowledge, but rather functions as an indicator of the limit of human knowledge. What does enter into the realm of our knowledge and ordinary language is a different type of nothing. To break the curse of Parmenides, Plato and his followers were approaching "what there is not" in the sense of "difference" or, in an Indian terminology, mutual nonbeing. As the absence or privation of being, this type of nothing is always an essential part of our knowledge. So the reason that we can think or talk about nonbeing or nothing with ease is not because Parmenides was wrong, but because we are approaching a different interpretation of nothing.

Leibniz was the first philosopher to put forward the perplexing metaphysical question: "Why is there something rather than nothing?" Various attempts to answer this question have understood nothing as an absolute nothing that is logically impossible. As a result, the existence of something is believed to have a higher probability or necessity. The question then becomes purely speculative, as if it is possible for a state of absolute nothing to exist prior to something. However, if we understand nothing in the Heideggerian or Daoist sense of original nothing, then the question is a matter of cosmogony, namely, how a concrete something with form and image comes about from a formless imageless state. To answer this, Christian theologians would resort to God's will, whereas the Daoists would rely on the creativity of *Dao*. In either case, nothing should not be understood as absolute nothing or absence; such an interpretation will lead to vain speculations. Instead, nothing is a formless, imageless state of existence, which is described as earth and water covered with darkness in the *Book of Genesis*, or simply as chaos in Daoist writings. It is only with this conception of nothing that we can make sense of this fundamental question of metaphysics.

I have expounded my typology of nothing by comparing the conceptions of nothing in Heidegger, Daoism, and Buddhism (three representative philosophical trends in the West, China, and India). Each has explored negativity to a great depth and preliminarily answers two perplexing questions in the philosophical discourse of nothing, that is, "why we cannot think or talk about nothing" and "why there is something rather than nothing." The depth of these discussions shows that it is wrong to indiscriminately exclude all kinds of nothing from the proper realm of philosophy. Instead, we should treat the subject more seriously by engaging with traditional sources in the East and West with the hope that we may eventually know better "what there is not."

NOTES

Chapter 1

1 *Samayabhedoparacanacakra*: 隨眠非心，非心所法，亦無所緣。隨眠異纏，纏異隨眠。應說隨眠與心不相應，纏與心相應。T2031: 15c28–16a1.

2 See *Samayabhedoparacanacakra*, T2031: 16c28–17a1.

3 See Yao (2005: 90n10).

4 *Samayabhedoparacanacakra*: 一切隨眠皆是心所，與心相應，有所緣境。一切隨眠皆纏所攝，非一切纏皆隨眠攝。T2031: 16b16–18.

5 For a discussion of the Sarvāstivāda theory of defilements based on these sources, see Dhammajoti (2007b: 418–79).

6 See Dhammajoti (2007b: 442–3).

7 See *Yibu zonglun lun shuji*, X844: 582b18–21. In his commentary on the *Kathāvatthu*, Buddhaghosa named seven types (see details later).

8 For the latter, more sources from the *Kathāvatthu* will be discussed later.

9 For the Saṃmatīya view, see Buddhaghosa's commentary on *Kathāvatthu* XI.1.

10 *Samayabhedoparacanacakra*: 一切隨眠皆是心所，與心相應。T2031: 16b16.

11 *Samayabhedoparacanacakra*: 亦無所緣。T2031: 15c28. The Tibetan translation reads: *dmigs pa med par (brjod par bya'o)*. P5639: 172a2.

12 *Samayabhedoparacanacakra*: 有所緣境。T2031: 16b16.

13 For the affiliation of the Andhakas and their sub-schools to the Mahāsāṃghikas, see Yao (2005: 23–5).

14 *Kathāvatthu* IX.4: *Saṅkhārakkhandho ekadeso sārammaṇo, ekadeso anārammaṇo ti.*

15 See *Kathāvatthu-aṭṭhakathā* IX. 4: *Anusayaṃ jīvitindriyaṃ kāyakammādirūpañ ca saṅkhārakkhandhapariyāpannaṃ, taṃ sandhāya paṭijānāti.*

16 See Lü (1991: 1964–5).

17 *Śāriputrābhidharma*: 云何一二分或心相應或非心相應？行陰是名一二分或心相 應或非心相應。. . . 云何行陰非心相應？行陰若非心數，生乃至滅盡定，是名行陰非心相應。T1548: 547b12–17. See also Dhammajoti (2007b: 373).

18 See *Kathāvatthu* IX.4, XI.1, and XIV.5.

19 See Yao (2005: 68–70).

20 In *Kathāvatthu* XI. 2, however, the Mahāsāṃghikas seem to argue that awareness should be inactive during this process.

21 See *Śāriputrābhidharma*, T1548: 590a7–8. Sanskrit words marked with * indicate that they are reconstructed on the basis of Chinese or Tibetan translations.

22 *Śāriputrābhidharma*: 云何無境界智？ 無境無境界智。T1548: 593c16–17.

23 Some editions of the text delete the second *jing* (境; object) to make this reading possible.

24 The Pāli Text Society edition of the *Kathāvatthu* and its English and Japanese translations separate the argument on the cognition of the future in an independent section IX.7. If examining the text more carefully, one would find it unnecessary to do so. This might be the reason that Buddhaghosa comments on the two sections together.

25 The English translator of the *Kathāvatthu* is therefore justified in rendering "*citta*" as "consciousness." See Shwe and Davids (1969 [*c.* 1915]: 237).

26 *Kathāvatthu* IX.6: *Atītārammaṇaṃ cittaṃ anārammaṇan ti*; IX. 7: *Anāgatārammaṇaṃ cittaṃ anārammaṇaṃ ti.*

27 *Kathāvatthu* IX.7: *atītānāgataṃ natthīti*. Here, I follow the Chaṭṭha Saṅgāyana CD (v. 3.0) edition. The Pāli Text Society edition reads: "*atītārammaṇaṃ n'atthīti*" (the past objects do not exist).

28 *Śāriputrābhidharma*: 云何無境界智？. . . 復次思惟過去未來法智生是名無境界智。T1548: 593c16–18.

29 See *Śāriputrābhidharma*, T1548: 701c10–11.

30 See *Śāriputrābhidharma*, T1548: 717a29–b2. I have to interpolate the character *jing* (境; object) to make this reading of the first definition possible. See section titled "Three Arguments" for further discussions.

31 See *Vijñānakāya*, T1539: 531a27–537a12.

32 See *Samayabhedoparacanacakra*, T2031: 16c26–27.

33 See *Samayabhedoparacanacakra*, T2031: 15b16–17.

34 *Vijñānakāya*: 有無所緣心。T1539: 535a8.

35 *Vijñānakāya*: 無所緣心決定是有。何者是耶？謂緣過去或緣未來。T1539: 535a19–20.

36 *Kathāvatthu* IX.4: *anusayā anārammaṇā*; *Samayabhedoparacanacakra*: 隨眠 . . . 亦無所緣。T2031: 15c28–29.

37 *Kathāvatthu* IX.5: *ñāṇaṃ anārammaṇan*.

38 *Śāriputrābhidharma*: 無境無境界智。T1548: 593c17.

39 *Kathāvatthu* IX.6: *atītānāgatārammaṇaṃ cittaṃ anārammaṇan.*

40 *Śāriputrābhidharma*: 思惟過去未來法智生, 是名無境界智。T1548: 593c17–18.

41 *Vijñānakāya*: 無所緣心決定是有, 何者是耶? 謂緣過去或緣未來。T1539: 535a19–20.

Chapter 2

1 For this Sanskrit reconstruction of the title *Cheng shi lun* (成實論), see Yao (2005: 98).

2 MV: 彼說有染與無染境，不決定故，知境非實。T1545: 288b18–19. The alternative translation AV (T1546: 223a24–25) reads: "they do not exist as fixed entities" (*wu you dingti* 無有定體). See Dhammajoti (2007a: 44) for his English translation.

3 MV: 由此故知境無實體。T1545: 288b27. The alternative translation AV (T1546: 223b3–4) reads: "do not exist as fixed entities" (*wu you dingti* 無有定體).

4 MV: 所系事是假。T1545: 288b16. The alternative translation AV (T1546: 223a22) reads: "Its cognitive sphere is unreal" (*chusuo shi jia*處所是假).

5 MV: 謂所有受不取外事而起分別，但依內事執取其相而起分別。T1545: 599b10–11. See Dhammajoti (2007a: 45) for his translation.

6 MV: 謂緣一切補特伽羅有， 緣法處所攝色、心不相應行、無爲法等名心受。T1545: 599b11–13. See Dhammajoti (2007a: 45) for his translation.

7 MV: 大徳欲令如是心受，無實境界，唯分別轉。T1545: 599b13–14. See Dhammajoti (2007a: 45) for his translation.

8 MV: 謂或有執，有緣無智，如譬喻者。彼作是說，若緣幻事、健達縛城及旋火輪、鹿愛等智，皆緣無境。T1545: 228b21–23.

9 MV: 謂或有執，有諸覺慧無所緣境。如取幻事、健達縛城、鏡像、水月、影光、鹿愛、旋火輪等種種覺慧，皆無實境。T1545: 558a8–10.

10 MV: 謂譬喻者作如是說，薩迦耶見無實所緣。彼作是言，薩迦耶見計我我所，於勝義中無我我所。如人見繩謂是蛇，見杌謂是人等。此亦如是，故無所緣。T1545: 36a17–20. AV (T1546: 26a18) has the Vibhajyavādas as the proponent of this view.

11 JP: 又所作幻事亦無而見有。T1646: 254a4–5.

12 JP: 知亦行於無所有處。T1646: 254a8–9.

13 JP: 知所行處名曰有相。T1646: 254a2–3.

14 JP: 有知無之知。T1646: 254c27.

15 MV: 即緣虛空非擇滅名。T1545: 42a21.

16 *Śāriputrābhidharma*: 云何無境界定？無無境界定。T1548: 717a29–b1.

17 *Śāriputrābhidharma*: 云何無境界智？無無境界智。T1548: 593c16–17, n18.

18 *Śāriputrābhidharma*: 云何無境界智？無境無境界智。T1548: 593c16–17. See the section titled 'Awareness without Objects' in Chapter 1 for further discussions.

19 NA: 又彼所言自相違害。謂說有覺非有為境，若覺有境，則不應言此境非有；若境非有，則不應言此覺有境。以非有者是都無故，若謂此覺境體都無，則應直言此覺無境。何所怯怖懷諂詐心矯說有覺非有為境？是故定無緣非有覺。T1562: 623b2–7.

20 *Śāriputrābhidharma*: 復次，思惟過去未來法若定生，是名無境界定。T1548: 717b1–2.

21 JP: 知亦行於無所有處，所以者何？如信解觀非青見青。... 又以知無所有故，名入無所有處定。T1646: 254a3–5.

22 NA: 譬喻論者作如是言：... 謂必應許非有亦能為境生覺。... 又有遍處等勝解作意故。 若一切 覺皆有所緣，是則應無勝解作意。T1562: 622a16–21.

23 NA: 勝解作意准此應知，謂瑜伽師見少相已，自勝解力於所見中，起廣行相生如是覺。此覺即緣諸蘊為境。T1562: 623b23–25.

24 JP: 是非青中實有青性。如經中說：「是木中有淨性。T1646: 254a28–29.

25 JP: 又汝言以知無所有，故名入無所有處定者。以三昧力故，生此無相，非是無也。如實有色，壞為空相。T1646: 254b3–5.

26 JP: 又入是三昧所見法少，故名為無。如鹽 少故名無鹽，慧少故名無慧。T1646: 254b5–7.

27 JP: 又汝言「如木中有淨性」者，是事不然，有因中有果過故。又汝言「取相心轉廣」者，是亦不然。本青相少，而見大地一切皆青，則是妄見。如是觀少青故，能見閻浮提盡皆是青，非妄見耶？... 又汝言「以三昧力故，生此無相，如實有色壞為空」者，若色實有而壞為空，則是顛倒。又「少而言無」，亦無（reads: 是）顛倒。T1646: 254c10–19.

28 NA: 有餘師說：... 此不淨觀，既是勝解作意所攝，理應名為顛倒作意，則應此觀體非是善。非此所緣，體皆是骨，皆作骨解，豈非顛倒？T1562: 672a10–15.

29 NA: 今觀行者作如是思：諸境界中，雖非皆骨，我今為伏諸煩惱故，應以勝解遍觀為骨。既隨所欲，如應而解，能伏煩惱，寧是顛倒？此觀勢力，能伏煩惱，令暫不行。既有如斯巧方便力，如何非善？是故無有如所難失。T1562: 672a28–b4.

30 *Kathāvatthu* V.3: *Paṭhavīkasiṇasamāpattiṃ samāpannassa viparīte ñāṇan ti?*

31 *Kathāvatthu* V.3: *Paṭhavīti samāpajjantassa sabb'eva paṭhavī hotīti?*

32 *Kathāvatthu-aṭṭhakathā* V.3: *Paṭhavin nissāya uppannanimittaṃ hi no paṭhavī yeva.*

33 *Kathāvatthu-aṭṭhakathā* V.3: *(Tato sakavādī) lakkhaṇapaṭhavī pi saṃbhārapaṭhavī pi nimittapaṭhavī pi paṭhavīdevatā pi sabbā paṭhavī yeva.*

Chapter 3

1 YBhc: 由此證有緣無意識。T1579: 585b4–5; YBht: *des na yid kyi rnam par shes pa med pa la dmigs pa ni yod pa kho nar khong du chud par bya ste* | D4038: zhi18a3.

2 YBhc: 由此故知意識亦緣非有為境。T1579: 585 a7–8.

3 YBht: *yid kyang med la dmigs pa yin par khong du chud par bya'o* || D4038: zhi17a4.

4 YBhc: 復有所餘如是種類言 論道理，證成定有緣無之識，如應當知。T1579: 585b5–6; YBht: *rnam par shes pa med pa la dmigs pa rab tu 'grub pa'i rigs pa brjod pa ni de lta bu dang mthun pa gzhan yang yod par rig par bya'o* || D4038: zhi18a3–4.

5 JDZL: 以是義故，定知諸識取無為境。T1584: 1022c29–1023a1.

6 JDZL: 眼識不得取無為境，心識云何能取無耶？T1584: 1022c9–10.

7 YBhc: 由彼意識亦緣去、來識為境界世現可得。T1579: 584c26–27; YBht: *'di ltar yid kyi rnam par shes pa ni 'das pa'i rnam par shes pa la dmigs pa yang yod* | *ma 'ongs pa'i rnam par shes pa la dmigs pa yang yod mod kyi* | D4038: zhi16b7.

8 YBhc: 如世尊言：過去諸行為緣生意，未來諸行為緣生意。T1579: 584c18–19; YBht: *bcom ldan 'das kyis yid ni 'das pa'i 'du byed rnams las kyang brten te 'byung la* | *yid ni ma 'ongs pa'i 'du byed rnams las kyang brten te 'byung ngo zhes gang gsungs pa de la* | D4038: zhi16b3.

9 How to understand and interpret the term "*dharma*" will be crucial to the second argument. For now, we can simply understand it as the object of mental consciousness.

10 YBhs 127,10: *sarvam iti yāvad eva dvādaśāyatanānīti* |

11 YBhs 127,13–14: *sarvam asti yāvad eva dvādaśāyatanānīti* |

12 YBhc: 由能執持諸五識身所不行義故，佛世尊假說名法。T1579: 584c23–24; YBht: *yid ni rnam par shes pa'i tshogs lnga po dag gi spyod yul ma yin pa'i don gang yin pa 'dzin par byed de* | *de la bcom ldan 'das kyis chos gdags par mdzad nas* | D4038: zhi16b5–6.

13 See Kuiji's commentary on YBh in T1829: 181b10–11.

14 YBhs 127,15–17: *sallakṣaṇā api dharmāḥ sallakṣaṇaṃ dhyārayanti* | *asallakṣaṇā api dharmā asallakṣaṇaṃ dhārayanti tasmād dharmā ity ucyante* |

15 YBhc: 又有性者，安立有義， 能持有義。若無性者，安立無義，能持無義。T1579: 584c28–29; YBht: *gzhan yang yod pa yang yod pa'i don gyis rnam par gnas shing yod pa'i don 'dzin par byed la | med pa yang med pa'i don gyis rnam par gnas shing med pa'i don 'dzin par byed pas* | D4038: zhi17a1.

16 YBhc: 由彼意識於有性義，若由此義而得安立，即以此義起識了別；於無性義，若由此義而得安立，即以此義起識了別。T1579: 584c29–585a3; YBht: *de la yid kyi rnam par shes pas ni yod pa yang don gang gis rnam par gnas pa'i don de nyid kyis rnam par shes par bya la | med pa yang don gang gis rnam par gnas pa'i don de nyid kyis rnam par shes par bya'o* || D4038: zhi17a1–2.

17 YBhc: 若於二種不 由二義起了別者，不應說意緣一切義、取一切義。T1579: 585a3–5; YBht: *gal te de gnyi ga gnyi ga'i don gyi[s] rnam par shes par mi byed na ni yid don thams cad la dmigs pa dang | don thams cad 'dzin pa yin par mi 'gyur ro* || D4038: zhi17a2–3. Correction following the Peking edition.

18 YBhs 127,17–18: *anyathā tu sato jñānād asataś ca ajñānād yogino na nirantarajñeyadharmaparīkṣā syād iti na yujyate* ||

19 The Sanskrit text of this passage is missing in YBhs. Its Chinese translation is found in YBhc: 又薄伽梵說：我諸無諂聲聞，如我所說，正修行時，若有知有，若無知無。T1579: 305a16–18; its Tibetan translation is found in YBht: *bcom ldan 'das kyis nyan thos g.yo med pa ni ngas gdams ngag byin te | yang dag par sgrub na | yod pa la yang yod par shes | med pa la yang med par shes so zhes gsungs pa gang yin pa* || D4035: dzi64a3.

20 YBhs 127,12–13: *sa ced apravṛttiṃ | tena yā nairātmyagrāhikā śaśaviṣāṇavandhyāputrādigrāhikā buddhir naivāstīti na yujyate* |

21 The term "*vaipulya*" could refer to one of the twelve divisions of the Buddhist canon. These twelve divisions include: (1) the Buddha's discourses (*sūtra*), (2) verses (*geya*), (3) the verse part of a discourse (*gāthā*), (4) historical narratives (*nidāna*), (5) activities of Buddha or his disciples in past lives (*itivṛttaka*), (6) Buddha's past life stories (*jātaka*), (7) Buddha's miraculous acts (*adbhutadharma*), (8) legends (*avadāna*), (9) didactic lessons (*upadeśa*), (10) teachings offered by the Buddha without prompting (*udāna*), (11) expanded teachings (*vaipulya*), and (12) guarantees of future attainment (*vyākaraṇa*). Alternatively, it could refer more generally to the Mahāyāna *sūtras*. It could also be associated with the Vetulyakas, and therefore linked to the Mahāsāṃghikas. But in Chapter 1 when we study the scattered Mahāsāṃghika sources on the cognition of nonexistent objects, no parallel was found between their arguments and these five arguments.

22 Here I follow closely the Tibetan translation. Xuanzang's translation (YBhc) conflates "cognition" with "consciousness," and reads: "The consciousness of universals does not arise without taking this object [of selflessness] as object."

23 YBhc: 如世尊微妙言說，若內、若外及二中間都無有我，此我無性非有為攝、非無為攝，共相觀識非不緣彼境界而轉。此名第一言論道理。T1579: 585a10–13; YBht: *bcom ldan 'das kyis legs par gsungs pa dang | legs par brjod pa ji skad du nang ngam phyi rol lam | lam gnyi ga la ma gtogs pa na bdag med do zhes gsungs pa gang yin*

pa de la | bdag med pa nyid de ni 'dus byas kyis bsdus pa yang ma yin 'dus ma byas kyis bsdus pa yang ma yin mod kyi | spyi'i mtshan nyid yongs su rtog pa rnams la de la dmigs pa'i rnam par shes pa mi 'byung ba yang ma yin te | de ltar na 'di ni rigs pa brjod pa dang po yin no || D4038: zhi17a5–7.

24 Here I follow closely the Tibetan translation. Xuanzang's translation (YBhc) conflates "cognition" with "consciousness," and reads: "The consciousness of universals does not arise without taking this object [of the very nature of impermanence, unstableness and non-eternality] as object."

25 YBhc: 又諸行中無常、無恒、無不變易，此諸行中常、恒、不變無性，非有為攝、非無為攝。共相觀識非不緣此境界而轉。……是名第四言論道理。T1579: 585a22–b2; YBht: *yang 'du byed thams cad la rtag pa nyid dam brtan pa nyid dam ther zug pa nyid med de 'du byed thams cad la rtag pa nyid dam brtan pa nyid dam ther zug nyid de'i med pa nyid de gang yin pa de yang 'dus byas kyis bsdus pa yang ma yin | 'dus ma byas kyis bsdus pa yang ma yin mod kyi | spyi'i mtshan nyid kyis yongs su rtog pa rnams la | de la dmigs pa'i rnam par shes pa mi 'byung ba yang ma yin te | … de ltar na 'di ni rigs pa brjod pa bzhi pa yin no* || D4038: zhi17b5–18a2.

26 BBh 276,17–18: *tatra saṃskṛtam asaṃskṛtaṃ ca sat | asad ātmā vā ātmīyaṃ vā* | See Dunnyun's commentary on YBh in T1828: 610a7–8.

27 See Dunnyun's commentary on YBh in T1828: 610a6–16.

28 For the relationship between yogic perception and other types of perception, see Yao (2005: 135–41).

29 Again, I follow the Tibetan translation. Xuanzang's translation (YBhc) reads: "The consciousness of particulars does not arise without taking this object [of the very nature of nonexistence] as object."

30 YBhc: 又於色、香、味、觸，如是如是生起變異，所安立中施設飲、食、車乘、衣服、嚴具、室宅、軍、林等事。此飲食等離色、香等都無所有，此無有性非有為攝、非無為攝，自相觀識非不緣彼境界而轉。是名第二言論道理。T1579: 585a13–17; YBht: *yang gzugs dang dri dang ro dang reg bya de lta de ltar byung ba rnams dang | yongs su gyur pa rnams dang | kun tu zhugs pa rnams la zas dang skom dang bzhon pa dang gos dang | rgyan dang khang khyim dang dmag dang nags tshal la sogs pa 'dogs par byed pa'i zas dang skom la sogs pa de dag gzugs la sogs pa las gud na cung zad kyang med de | de'i med pa nyid gang yin pa de yang 'dus byas kyis bsdus pa yang ma yin | 'dus ma byas kyis bsdus pa yang ma yin | mod kyi rang gi mtshan nyid yongs su rtog pa rnams la | de la dmigs pa'i rnam par shes pa mi 'byung ba yang ma yin te | de ltar na 'di ni rigs pa brjod pa gnyis pa yin no* || D4038: zhi17a7–b2.

31 The Sarvāstivādins accept one more material element called "unmanifested form" (*avijñaptirūpa*), while the Yogācāras accept instead five more kinds of material form called "material thought-objects" (*dharmāyatanikāni rūpāni*).

32 Kuiji's commentary on the *Nyāyapraveśa*: 若許有體，不證緣無。T1840: 138c23–24.

33 See Kuiji's commentary on YBh in T1829: 181c3–5.

34 See Paramārtha's translation of JDZL in T1584: 1022c17–18.

35 I did not get a chance to discuss the fifth and final rational discourse of *vaipulya*, which says: "Again, the future phenomena have not arisen yet, how can there be their cessation? But it is not the case that the sagely disciples do not abide in observing the arising and cessation of future phenomena. This is the fifth rational discourse." (YBhc: 又未來行尚無有生，何況有滅？然聖弟子於未來行，非不隨觀生滅而住。是名第五言論道理。T1579: 585b2–4; YBht: *yang 'du byed ma 'ongs pa rnams kyi 'byung ba nyid kyang re zhig med na 'jig pa yod par lta ga la 'gyur* | *yang 'phags pa nyan thos rnams 'du byed ma 'ongs pa rnams la 'byung ba dang* | *'jig par rjes su lta zhing mi gnas pa yang ma yin te* | *de ltar na 'di ni rigs pa brjod pa lnga pa yin no* || D4038: zhi18a2–3.) Since it discusses future phenomena, it can be taken as part of argument 1.

36 The Tibetan translation reads: "Suppose that the non-existence-ness (*med pa nyid*) of the nonexistence (*med pa*) of wish, worship, etc. really is an existent" (*gal te 'dod pa dang mchod sbyin la sogs pa med pa'i med pa nyid gang yin pa de yang dag par yod pa nyid yin na ni*). The omission of "donation" supports an alternative edition of Xuanzang's translation (YBhc) which also skips "donation."

37 The interpolation of "that there exist soul (*puruṣa*) and person (*pudgala*)" (*skyes bu gang zag*) is based on the Tibetan translation.

38 The Tibetan translation omits this interrogation.

39 This is the best way I can formulate this difficult sentence. The Tibetan translation seems to suggest the arising of the non-arising of the heretic's consciousness: "*ci ste med na ni log par lta ba rnams kyi de la dmigs pa'i rnam par shes pa yang 'byung bar mi 'gyur ba zhig na 'byung ste.*"

40 YBhc: 又撥一切都無所有邪見，謂無施、無愛、亦無祠祀，廣說如前。若施、愛、祠等無性是有，即如是見應非邪見，何以故？彼如實見如實說故。此若是無，諸邪見者緣此境界，識應不轉。是名第三言論道理。T1579: 585a18–22; YBht: *yang na thams cad la skur ba 'debs pa'i log par lta ba ji skad du sbyin pa med do* || *'dod pa med do* || *mchod sbyin med do zhes rgya cher sngar bstan pa lta bu gang yin pa de la* | *gal te 'dod pa dang mchod sbyin la sogs pa med pa'i med pa nyid gang yin pa de yang dag par yod pa nyid yin na ni des na skyes bu gang zag de lta bur lta ba de yang log par lta bar mi 'gyur te* | *'di ltar de ni yang dag par lta ba dang* | *yang dag par smra bar 'gyur ro* || *ci ste med na ni log par lta ba rnams kyi de la dmigs pa'i rnam par shes pa yang 'byung bar mi 'gyur ba zhig na 'byung ste* | *de ltar na de ni rigs pa brjod pa gsum pa yin no* || D4038: zhi17b2–5.

41 YBhs 151,21: *sarvaṃ sarvalakṣaṇena nāstīti* | 153,3: *nāsti sarvaṃ sarvalakṣaṇena iti* |

42 For further discussions on the adverbialist theory, the object view, and the existent-object view of intentionality, see Kriegel (2008).

Chapter 4

1 See especially Kritzer (2005) and Dhammajoti (2007a: 5–40).

2 See AKBh 295,10–13. This *sūtra* is included as No. 79 of the *Saṃyukta Āgama*, see T99: 20a10–24.

3 AKBh 295,16–17: *dvayaṃ pratītya vijñānasyotpāda iti uktaṃ dvayaṃ katamat | cakṣū rūpāṇi yāvat mano dharmā iti |* Similar passages can be found in No. 214 of the *Saṃyukta Āgama*, T99: 54a22–b1 and the *Saṃyutta Nikāya*, 35,93.

4 AK 5.25b: *sadviṣayāt . . .* |

5 AKBh 295,20–21: *sati viṣaye vijñānaṃ pravartate nāsati | yadi cātītānāgataṃ na syād, asadālambanaṃ vijñānaṃ syāt | tato vijñānam eva na syād ālambanābhāvāt |*

6 Vibhajyavāda is a general title assigned to those who argued against the Sarvāstivāda view of the existence of the past and the future. For the Kāśyapīya view, see Vasumitra's *Samayabhedoparacanacakra*, T2031: 17a27–b2.

7 La Vallée Poussin (1971: 55): "Le Sautrāntika critique . . ." See Puguang's commentary in T1821: 311b17ff and Fabao's in T1822: 704a7ff.

8 See, for instance, Kritzer (2005: xxvi–xxx).

9 AK 1.17ab: *ṣaṇṇām anantarātītaṃ vijñānaṃ yad dhi tan manaḥ |* "Of the six consciousnesses, the one which continually passes away, is the *manas*."

10 AKBh 299,20–21: *kiṃ tasya yathā mano janakaḥ pratyaya evaṃ dharmā āhosvid ālambanamātraṃ dharmā iti |*

11 AKVy 474,13: *na hi pūrvakālīnasya phalasya paścātkālīno hetur yujyata iti . . .* |

12 NA: 若謂"意根與所生識，一類相續，無間引生，可名能生。法不爾"者 . . . T1562: 628a9–10.

13 See NA T1562: 628a10–12.

14 NA: 意為意識所依 生緣，法為所緣能生意識。所依緣別，生緣義同。T1562: 628a5–7.

15 AKBh 299,23: *sarvapravṛttinirodhā[t] . . .* |

16 AKVy 474,14: *nirvāṇaṃ hi vijñānaṃ niruddhān na janayet . . .* |

17 JP: 但遮計神，故如是說：若諸識生，皆由此二，非四因緣。T1646: 364a18–19.

18 JP: 佛破神我，故說二法因緣生識，非盡然也。T1646: 254b19–20. ("For the purpose of refuting self, the Buddha speaks of a consciousness arising on the basis of two conditions. But it is not necessarily true.")

19 *Tattvasaṃgrahapañjikā* 630,16–18: *dvividhaṃ hi vijñānan sālambanam anālambanam ca | yat sālambanaṃ tad abhisandhāya dvyāśrayavijñānadeśanā bhagavataḥ ||*

20 AKBh 299,23–24: *atha ālambanamātraṃ dharmā bhavanti | atītānāgatam apy ālambanaṃ bhavatīti brūmaḥ |*

21 AKBh 299,7: *astiśabdasya nipātatvāt |*

22 Alternatively, the past exists (*asti*) and the future exists (*asti*).

23 Alternatively, [the past and the future] exist (*asti*).

24 AKBh 299,1–3: *vayam api brūmo 'sty atītānāgatam iti | atītaṃ tu yad bhūtapūrvam | anāgataṃ yat sati hetau bhaviṣyati | evaṃ ca kṛtvā 'stīty ucyate na tu punar dravyataḥ |*

25 Xuanzang's translation of AKBh: 有聲通顯有無法。T1558: 105b12.

26 AKBh 299,11: *yat karmābhyatītaṃ kṣīṇaṃ niruddhaṃ vigataṃ vipariṇataṃ tad asti . . .* | Original source cannot be identified. Yaśomitra refers to the *Saṃyukta Āgama* when discussing this passage, see AKVy 473,16.

27 AKBh 299,13: *anyathā hi svena bhāvena vidyamānam atītaṃ na sidhyet |*

28 AKBh 299,14–16: *cakṣur utpadyamānaṃ na kutaścid āgacchati nirudhyamānaṃ na kvacit saṃnicayaṃ gacchati | iti hi bhikṣavaś cakṣur abhūtvā bhavati bhūtvā ca prativigacchatīti* [Pradhan: *pratigacchatīti*] | (My corrections of Pradhan's edition of AKBh follow Odani and Honjō (2007: Appendix 15–19), except for a few occasions.) An abridged Chinese translation of the *Paramārthaśūnyatāsūtra* is included as No. 335 of the *Saṃyukta Āgama* (T99: 92c12–26), and the quoted passage is found in T99: 92c16–17. The complete Chinese translation of this short *sūtra* was made available later (T655: 806c23–807a20).

29 For the importance of this *sūtra* to Vasubandhu's AKBh, see Miyashita (1986).

30 AKBh 299,24: *yadi nāsti katham ālambanam |*

31 AKBh 299,25: *yathā* [Pradhan: *yadā*] *tadālambanaṃ tathāsti |*

32 See NA, T1562: 628b11–14.

33 AKBh 299,26–27: *yathā khalv api vart* [Pradhan: *tt*]*amānaṃ rūpam anubhūtaṃ tathā tad atītaṃ smaryate |*

34 AKBh 299,28–29: *yadi ca tat tathā eva asti vartmānaṃ prāpnoti | atha nāsti | asad apy ālambanaṃ bhavatīti siddham |*

35 See NA, T1562: 628b14–20.

36 See especially NA, T1562: 622a16–27. For contemporary studies, see Sakamoto (1981: 142–50) and Cox (1988: 49–55).

37 NA: 若如現有追憶過去，而說彼有如成所緣，是則極成過去實有。 以如現在領實有相，如是追憶過去為有。既許彼有如所追憶，如何過去體非實有？ T1562: 628b20–24.

38 AKBh 300,9–10: *yaś ca śabdasya prāgabhāvam ālambate kiṃ tasyālambanam |*

39 See NA, T1562: 622a25–26.

40 AKBh 300,10–11: *yaḥ śabdābhāvaṃ prārthayate, tasya śabda eva kartavyaḥ syāt* |

41 AKBh 300,13: *ubhayaṃ vijñānasyālambanaṃ bhāvaś cābhāvaś ca* |

42 NA: 此中緣聲先非有識，緣聲依處，非即緣聲。謂但緣聲所依眾具，未發聲位，為聲非有。T1562: 624b18–20.

43 NA: 諸互非有，定依有說。T1562: 624b15. See also T1562: 431b23.

44 NA: 若不然者，應體非燈。T1562: 636a22.

45 NA: 謂去來世，體有用無。 T1562: 636a23.

46 NA: 體謂去來所知法性，有所知性，故說為有。T1562: 636a23–24.

47 AKBh 300,1: *vikīrṇasyāgrahaṇāt* |

48 AKBh 300,3: *na tu kiṃcid utpadyate nāpi nirudhyata . . .* |

49 AKBh 300,6–7: *atha na santi* | *asad apy ālambanam iti siddham* |

50 AKBh 300,7–8: *yady asad apy ālambanaṃ syāt, trayodaśam apy āyatanaṃ syāt* |

51 NA: 又彼所言自相違害。謂說有覺非有為境，若覺有境，則不應言此境非有；若境非有，則不應言此覺有境。以非有者是都無故，若謂此覺境體都無，則應直言此覺無境。何所怯怖懷諂詐心，矯說有覺非有為境？是故定無緣非有覺。T1562: 623b2–7.

52 AKBh 300,8: *atha trayodaśam āyatanaṃ nāstīty asya vijñānasya kim ālambanam* |

53 AKBh 300,9: *etad eva nāmālambanam* |

54 See MV, T1545: 42a29. The other four types of existence are real (**dravyasat*, *shiyou* 實有), conventional (**prajñatisat* or **saṃvṛtisat*, *jiayou* 假有), composite (**saṃghātasat* or **sāmagrīsat*, *heheyou* 和合有), and reciprocal existences (**anyonyasat* or **apekṣāsat*, *xiangdaiyou* 相待有).

55 AKBh 300,14–15: *yal*[Pradhan: *yat tat*] *loke nāsti tad ahaṃ jñāsyāmi vā drakṣyāmi vā nedaṃ sthānaṃ vidyata iti* |

56 See JP, T1646: 254a20 and *Abhidharmadīpa* 269,7. For the authorship of the *Abhidharmadīpa*, see Li (2013).

57 *Madhyama Āgama*: 若世中無是，我可見可知彼耶？ T26: 536c27–28. Its parallel is not found in the Pāli *Upakkilesa Sutta* (No. 128 of the *Majjhima Nikāya*), which corresponds to this Chinese *sūtra*.

58 AKBh 300,15–16: *apare ābhimānikā bhavanty asantam apy avabhāsaṃ santaṃ paśyanti* | *ahaṃ tu santam evāstīti paśyāmi . . .* |

59 AKBh 300,16–17: *sarvabuddhīnāṃ sadālambanatve . . .* |

60 NA: 故一切覺皆緣有境，由此於境得有猶豫，謂我於此所見境中，為是正知，為是顛倒。T1562: 622c22–24.

61 AKBh 300,18–21: *etu*[Pradhan: *etat*] *bhikṣur mama śrāvako yāvat sa mayā kalyam*[Pradhan: *kalpam*] *avoditaḥ sāyaṃ viśeṣāya paraiṣyati* | *sāyam avoditaḥ kalyaṃ*[Pradhan: *kalpaṃ*] *viśeṣāya paraiṣyati* | *sac ca satto jñāsyaty asac cāsattaḥ*[Pradhan: *sacca sato jñāsyati asaccāsataḥ*] *sottaraṃ ca sottarataḥ anuttaraṃ cānuttarata*[Pradhan: *cānurattarata*] *iti* | See No. 703 of the *Saṃyukta Āgama*, T99: 189a20–b9 and the *Aṅguttara Nikāya* 10,22.

62 See Chapter 3. Its Chinese translation is found in T1579: 305a16–18 and Tibetan translation in D4035: dzi64a3.

63 See NA, T1562: 623a3–4.

Chapter 5

1 Based on the available sources, we can roughly assume that Kumārila was an elder contemporary of Dharmakīrti. Īśvarasena, being the teacher of Dharmakīrti, was certainly earlier than the latter. But we do not know for sure whether he was earlier than Kumārila, or whether he was influenced by the latter. Neither can we sufficiently explain why the issue of non-cognition attracted so much attention in the seventh century.

2 This sixfold classification of *pramāṇa* was known to the seventh-century Chinese scholar Kuiji, who rendered the sixth *pramāṇa* as *wutiliang* (無體量), see T1840: 95b18.

3 The other two types of evidence are effect (*kārya*) and identity (*svabhāva*), both of which guarantee the necessity of affirmative judgments.

4 See the *Nyāyapraveśa* 7,11–12: *ātmapratyāyanārthaṃ tu pratyakṣam anumānaṃ ca dve eva pramāṇe* || … *kalpanājñānam arthāntare* ***pratyakṣābhāsam*** | … *hetvābhāsapūrvakaṃ jñānam* ***anumānābhāsam*** | …

5 似現似比，總入非量。由此可言，現量非比及非非量，比量亦是非非量攝。T1840: 95c16–17.

6 See T1585: 10b20–c4. On one occasion, La Vallée Poussin (1928–29: 134) translates *feiliang* into non-*pramāṇa*.

7 On the basis of Ono et al. (1996), it can be determined that *apramāṇatva* appears three times and *apramāṇatā* eight times in the extant Sanskrit works of Dharmakīrti. But their meaning in PV III.86, 88, and 99 is apparently different from that found elsewhere.

8 PV III.85ab: *pratiṣedhas tu sarvatra sādhyate 'nupalambhataḥ* |

9 PV III.86: *dṛṣṭā viruddhadharmoktis tasya tatkāraṇasya vā* | *niṣedhe yā 'pi tasyaiva sā 'pramāṇatvasūcanā* ||

10 PV III.89b: *sā 'bhāvasya prasādhikā* |

11 PV III.99: *yad apramāṇatā 'bhāve liṅgaṃ tasyaiva kathyate* | *tad atyantavimūḍhārthaṃ āgopālam asaṃvṛtteḥ* ||

12 PVV 83,7–8: *yad evādarśanaṃ sā 'pramāṇatā pramāṇarahitatā 'nupalabhir* ... ||

13 See PVV 82,22 and 85,6.

14 See PV III.88cd: *dṛśyasya darśanābhāvād iti cet sā 'pramāṇatā* ||

15 PV III.94: *aniścayakaraṃ proktam īdṛk[ṣ]ānupalambhanam* | *tatrātyantaparokṣeṣu sadasattāviniścayau* || Correction following Tosaki (1979: 169).

16 See Katsura (1992: 231). The relevant passage in the *Nyāyamukha* reads: 夫立宗法，理應更以餘法為因成立此法。若即成立有法為有，或立為無，如有成立「最勝為有，現見別物有總類故」；或立「為無，不可得 故」，其義云何？此中但立「別物定有一因」為宗，不立「最勝」，故無此失。若立「為無」，亦假安立「不可得」法，是故亦無有有法過。T1628: 1b27–c4. But in the *Pramāṇasamuccayavṛtti*, chapter three, it is revised as follows: *chos can yang des min* | *chose kyi(s) chos can yang bsgrub pa ma yin te* (|) *dper na gtso bo gcig yod pa yin te* | *khyad par rnams la rjes su 'gro ba mthong ba'i phyir ro zhes bya ba lta bu'o* || *de ni khyad par rmans kho na rgyu gcig pa can nyid du bsgrub par bya ba yin te* | *der yang gyo mo la sogs pa'i rgyu gcig pa nyid dper byed pa yin no* || *de'i phyir chos gzhan kho na bsgrub par bya ba yin no* || P5702: 128b6–8. See Chapter 6 for further discussions on these passages.

17 空等畢竟物不可得，猶如兔角，畢竟如是六根各各皆不能得。如是空等亦不可得，是故知無。T1565: 48a7–9.

18 See the *Ślokavārttika abhāva* 4–5. The other three are prior nonexistence (*prāgabhāva*), posterior nonexistence (*dhvaṃsa*), and mutual nonexistence (*anyonyābhāva*). This way of classification is also referred to by Śāntarakṣita in his *Tattvasaṃgraha* 1650–4.

19 法身應決定是無，不可執故。若物非六識所得，決定是無，如兔角。兔角者，非六識所得，定是無故。法身亦爾，是故法身決定是無。T1610: 803c21–24.

20 汝言「非六識所見故法身無」者，是義不然。何以故？以由方便能證涅槃故。想稱正行，是名方便。由此方便，是故法身可知可見。譬如由他心通故，則能得見出世聖心。T1610: 803c24–28.

21 For different opinions regarding the date of Asvabhāva and his relationship to Dignāga, see Tsukamoto et al. (1990: 291–2). One of the major pieces of evidence for Asvabhāva having been familiar with Dignāga is that he mentioned the famous theory of Dignāga that cognition is divided into three parts: "There are multiple aspects within the unity of consciousness: self-awareness, subject and object. These three aspects" (MSṬ 298b8: *shes pa gcig nyid rnam pa mang por rang gis rig go* | *rtog pa rnam pa 'di gsum rnam par* ...). The Chinese reads: 又於一識似三相現，所取、能取及自證分，名為三相。T1598: 415b28–29. For a further discussion of this passage, see Yao (2006).

22 「如顯現非有」者，我性、法性、所取、能取，如是等體，皆無有性，非量所證，故說為無。T1598: 408a18–20. The Tibetan translation is slightly different: "'Like they appear, [they] do not exist.' [This means:] Self, *dharma*, grasper and grasped do not exist in reality because there is no means of cognition (*tshad ma med pa*) [for their existence in reality]." (MSṬ 284b4–5: *ji ltar snang ba de bzhin med ces bya ba ni bdag dang chos sam gzung ba dang 'dzin pa'i dngos por med pa nyid de* | *tshad ma med pa'i phyir ro* |) The Tibetan suggests an alternative reading of the Chinese translation: "... because [they are] not (*fei*) what is cognized by a means of cognition (*liang-suo-zheng*量所證), so [they are] regarded as nonexistent." Before we find the Sanskrit text, this passage remains inconclusive to support my interpretation.

23 MSṬ 258b8–259a1: *de lta bas na 'dir ni dmigs pa la mi dmigs pa yongs su gcod pa yin kyi med pa nyid ni ma yin te* | *'di ltar de'i tshe chos med pa ni ma yin gyi* | *yod bzhin du yongs su* | *mi gcod do* | The Chinese reads: 如是，此中但說「所緣為不可得」，難了知故，非全無有。以於爾時非無有法，雖是其有，而不可知。T1598: 393a5–7.

24 又以五識同現量攝，故合立一，說在最初。餘識不定，或現或比或非量攝，故別立一，說在第二。T1580: 886a7–9.

25 破極微中，有五徵難。初中若已觀察違諸量故者，現比二量所不得故，猶如兔角，定非實有。彼宗雖計現量所得，此宗說非量知。迴色但有阿拏以上麤色，現量可得，非極微故。T1828: 349a23–27. Buddhist philosophers believed that a molecule (*aṇu*) usually consists of seven atoms.

26 謂八識量總有三種：一者現量，現謂現前，量謂量度。謂於現前明了色等，不迷亂相而得了知，離諸名言種類分別，照鏡明白，故名現量。現即是量，持業釋也；二者比量，比謂比類，量義同前。謂於不現在前色等，而藉眾-相於所觀義有正智生，了知有大或無常等，是名比量。比即是量，亦持業釋；三者非量，謂若有境，非可現知明白而照，亦非眾緣而可比度，境體實無，非可量度。於非量處而起心量，故名非量，故非六釋。T2810: 1053a8–17. Six types of Sanskrit compounds were known to medieval Chinese Buddhist scholars: *dvandva*, *tatpuruṣa*, *karmadhāraya*, *dvigu*, *avyayībhāva*, and *bahuvrīhi*.

27 若後得智亦通三量等者，緣自相故，是現量智；緣共相故，是比量智；緣過未故，是非量智。T2812: 1078a8–9.

28 For that matter, we should also include Dunnyun to the list.

Chapter 6

1 *Nyāyamukha*: [問] 若即成立有法為有，或立為無。如有成立「最勝為有，現見別物有總類故」；或立「為無，不可得故」，其義云何？[答] 此中但立「別物定有一因」為宗，不立「最勝」，故無此失；若立「為無」，亦假安立「不可得」法，是故亦無有有法過。T1628: 1b27–c4. The partial Sanskrit reconstruction is

based on Dharmakīrti's reference in his *Pramāṇavārttikasvavṛtti* 105, 107. See Katsura (1992: 230) for his English translation and Tillemans (1999: 174–5) for his discussion of the passage.

2 Huizhao (慧沼; 651–714), his disciple Zhizhou (智周; 668–723), and his master Kuiji (632–82) were considered to be the three patriarchs of the Faxiang-Yogācāra school. Huizhao's works on Buddhist logic include two commentaries on the *Nyāyapraveśa*.

3 *Pramāṇasamuccayavṛtti*: *dper na gtso bo gcig yod pa yin te | khyad par rnams la rjes su 'gro ba mthong ba'i phyir ro zhes bya ba lta bu'o || de ni khyad par rmans kho na rgyu gcig pa can nyid du bsgrub par bya ba yin te | der yang gyo mo la sogs pa'i rgyu gcig pa nyid dper byed pa yin no* || P5702: 128b6–8.

4 Shentai (神泰; active 645–58) was a disciple of Xuanzang. His work on Buddhist logic is his commentary on the *Nyāyamukha*.

5 *Limenlun shuji*: 此中二十三諦別物，定有一総因 宗；以是別故 因；猶如多片白檀同喻。 T1839: 82a13–15.

6 *Limenlun shuji*: 二十三諦無有一最勝因 宗；以最勝不可得故 因；猶如菟角同喻。T1839: 82a18–19. Among Sanskrit, Tibetan, and Chinese sources, S2 is the only instance we have found so far that explicitly tackles the problem of the negative proposition by using the method of paraphrasing.

7 PV I.212: *śabdārthaḥ kalpanājñānaviṣayatvena kalpitaḥ | dharmo vastvāśrayāsiddhir asyokto nyāyavādinā* ||

8 PV I.206: *tasmin bhāvānupādāne sādhye 'syānupalambhanam | tathā hetur na tasyaivābhāvaḥ śabdaprayogataḥ* ||

9 Russell (1994: 418): "But the chief objection is that such objects, admittedly, are apt to infringe the law of contradiction. It is contended, for example, that the present King of France exists, and also does not exist; that the round square is round, and also not round, etc."

10 *Yinming ru zhengli lun yi zuanyao*: 若許有體， 不可言無，自語相違。 T1842: 162c14–15.

11 See the next section for further discussion on this issue.

12 MV T1545: 42a29–b4. The other four types of existence are real (**dravyasat*, 實有), conventional (**prajñaptisat* or **saṃvṛtisat*, 假有), composite (**saṃghātasat* or **sāmagrīsat*, 和合有), and reciprocal existences (**anyonyasat* or * *apekṣāsat*, 相待有). For further sources on the Sarvāstivāda notions of existence, see Dhammajoti (2007b: 76–86).

13 Matilal seems to be the first one to have used the term "pan-fictionalism" to indicate the position of a Buddhist opponent in Nyāya works. Funayama (1991) suggests that this position was associated with Jñānaśrīmitra and Ratnakīrti, but as we have discussed, it can actually be traced back to Dharmakīrti or even Dignāga himself. See Siderits (1991) for further discussions.

14 A lag sha ngag dbang bstan dar, *gCig du bral gyi rnam bzhag*, §2. Ngag dbang bstan dar (1759–1840) was a dGe lugs pa scholar from the A la shan region of Inner Mongolia. He treated this issue in his *gCig du bral gyi rnam bzhag*, a Madhyamaka work on various problems centered around the Svātantrika Madhyamaka's use of the "neither one nor many reason" (*ekānekaviyogahetu*) for emptiness. The Tibetan text of relevant sections is included in Tillemans (1999: 258–65), and its English translation by Tillemans and Lopez is found in Tillemans (1999: 249–58).

15 *Nyāyamukha*: 前是遮詮，後唯止濫。T1628: 2c8–9. It corresponds to the following passage in the *Pramāṇasamuccayavṛtti*: *snga ma ni ma yin par dgag pa yin la phyi ma ni med par dgag pa yin par brjod do* | P5701: 64a4 (cf. P5702: 148b2 and D4204: 60a6–7). See Kitagawa (1965: 242, n498) and Katsura (1981: 63).

16 *pradhānatvaṃ vidher yatra pratiṣedhe 'pradhānatā | paryudāsaḥ sa vijñeyo yatrottarapadena nañ* || According to Edgerton (1986: 167, n219), this verse and the verse in the following note are quoted from the *Vākyapadīya* of Bhartṛhari, but they are not found in its received version. See Matilal (1968: 157) for his translation and discussion.

17 *aprādhānyaṃ vidher yatra pratiṣedhe pradhānatā | prasajya-pratiṣedho 'yaṃ kriyayā saha yatra nañ* || Matilal (1968: 157) reads *'yaṃ* as *'sau*.

18 A lag sha ngag dbang bstan dar, *gCig du bral gyi rnam bzhag*, section 2, English translation from Tillemans (1999: 250).

19 *Yinming ru zhengli lun yi zuanyao*: 及因有體，表而亦遮，必依有體有法 . . . 其因無體，但遮非表，以無為依。故非無依，及成有法過。T1842: 162c17–20. The same phrase "a negation that implies no affirmation" (*dan zhe fei biao*但遮非表) was discussed by Kuiji who explained it with the example "the self does not exist" (T1840: 135c3–4).

20 A lag sha ngag dbang bstan dar, *gCig du bral gyi rnam bzhag*, sections 2–3; see Tillemans (1999: 250–1).

21 Kuiji was the most important disciple of Xuanzang and a key player in the formation of Faxiang-Yogācāra school in China. He composed numerous commentaries on the works translated by his master. For his view on this point, see Shen (2002: 147ff.). For the life and works of Kuiji, see Lusthaus (2002: 382ff.).

22 The classical source for the discussion of this method is found in Kuiji's commentary on the *Nyāyapraveśa* (T1840). For contemporary studies, see Shen (2002: 166–96), Harbsmeier (1998: 392–6), and Frankenhauser (1996: 88–90).

23 *Limenlun shuji*:: 汝所計最勝是無 宗；不可得故 因；猶如菟角喻。T1839: 82a24–25.

24 This probably started with Kamalaśīla's *Madhayamakāloka*. See Tillemans (1999: 271–2, n13).

25 See Kuiji's commentary on the *Nyāyapraveśa* T1840: 115b21–28 and 121b25–c13. Kuiji reports that Jayasena (*sheng-jun* 勝軍) was also known by the honorific title Prasenajit (*bao-cuo-jia* 抱蹉迦, T1840: 121b19). For the most recent study of Xuanzang's "mind-only" inference, see Franco (2004), who explained this inference with great clarity, but did not treat the phrase "we accept."

26 See Dharmapāla's commentary on Āryadeva's *Catuḥśataka*: "Therefore the past and the future that are accepted by both you and us do not exist independent of the present, because it is included in the [three] times that *is accepted by us*, like the present." (由此去來共所許法，非離現在別有實體，自宗所許世所攝故，猶如現在。T1571: 215a3–4.)

27 Graham Priest (personal communication, October 5, 2007) comments that the most effective solution to the problem of empty terms is the Meinongian approach.

Chapter 8

1 For more examples, see May (1996: 21–6).

2 Heidegger (1990: 271). Cited from Wirtz (2006: 333). My translation. For more discussions on this concept, see Kwan (1982: 76, 83–4, and 142).

3 See Kant (1956: 332–3). The other two types are rational entity (*ens rationis*) and imaginary entity (*ens imaginarium*).

4 See Kobusch (1984: 809). The other three types are negation, mutual relation, and the not-yet existent (*Noch-nichtsein*). Another Neo-Platonist Ammonios Hermeiou added the fifth ineffable unrepresentable nothing to the list.

5 For instance, Liu (1997: 159), Wang (2001: 155), and Lin (2007: 151).

6 I exclude chapter 1, because I read the relevant sentence there as "the nameless (*wuming* 無名) is the origin of heaven and earth" rather than "nothing (*wu* 無) is called (*ming* 名) the origin of heaven and earth."

7 See the *Mo-Jing* and its commentary: 無不必待有，... 無天陷，則無之而無 (Nothing does not necessarily presuppose being ... In the case the nothing of the sky's falling down, it is nothing without ever having been).

8 *Dao-De-Jing*, chapter 40: 天下萬物生於有，有生於無。

9 *Zhuang-Zi*, chapter of Geng-Sang-Chu:
萬物出乎無有，有不能以有為有，必出乎無有，而無有一無有。

10 *Dao-De-Jing*, chapter 2: 有無相生。

11 It is found in the encyclopedic YBh (T1579: 362c19–20) and its commentaries (T1828: 416a15–16 and T1829: 97a25–26).

12 *Mūlamadhyamakakārikā* 15.1–2: *na saṃbhavaḥ svabhāvasya yuktaḥ pratyayahetubhiḥ | hetupratyayasaṃbhūtaḥ svabhāvaḥ kṛtako bhavet || svabhāvaḥ kṛtako nāma bhaviṣyati punaḥ kathaṃ | akṛtrimaḥ svabhāvo hi nirapekṣaḥ paratra ca ||*

13 *Mūlamadhyamakakārikā* 24.18ab: *yaḥ pratītyasamutpādaḥ śūnyatāṃ tāṃ pracakṣmahe |*

14 *Mūlamadhyamakakārikā* 24.18c: *sā prajñaptir upādāya pratipat . . .||*

15 Contemporary scholars with this approach are represented by Eugene Burnouf, H. Jacobi, M. Walleser, I. Wach, A. B. Keith, and La Vallee Poussin. See Lin (1999: 183–6).

16 Contemporary representatives of this approach are St. Schayer, Stcherbatsky, and Murti. See Lin (1999, 186–91).

17 *Mūlamadhyamakakārikā* 24.18d: *saiva madhyamā ||*

18 See Piṅgala's commentary on the *Mūlamadhyamakakārikā*, T1564: 33b17.

19 *Majjhima-nikāya* III.104: *iti yaṃ hi kho tattha na hoti, tena taṃ suññaṃ samanupassati, yaṃ pana tattha avasiṭṭhaṃ hoti, taṃ santaṃ idaṃ atthīti pajānāti.*

20 *Madhyāntavibhāga* I.13ab: *dvayābhāvo hy abhāvasya bhāvaḥ śūnyasya lakṣaṇaṃ |*

21 See the relevant studies in Luo (2003) and Zhao (2007).

REFERENCES

Primary Sources (With Abbreviations)

Abhidharmadīpa with *Vibhāṣāprabhāvṛtti* of Īśvara. *Abhidharmadīpa with Vibhāṣāprabhāvṛtti*, edited by P. S. Jaini, 2nd edn, Tibetan Sanskrit Works Series 4. Patna: K.P. Jayaswal Research Institute, 1977.

AK(Bh): *Abhidharmakośa* (AK) and *-bhāṣya* (AKBh) of Vasubandhu. *Abhidharmakośabhāṣya of Vasubandhu*, edited by P. Pradhan, 2nd edn, Tibetan Sanskrit Works Series 8. Patna: K.P. Jayaswal Research Institute, 1975.

AKVy: *Sphuṭārthā Abhidharmakośavyākhyā* of Yaśomitra. *Sphuṭārthā Abhidharmakośavyākhyā: The Work of Yaśomitra*, edited by Unrai Wogihara. Tokyo: The Publishing Association of Abhidharmakośavyākhyā, Sankibo Buddhist Book Store, [1936] 1989.

Aṅguttara Nikāya. *The Aṅguttara-Nikāya*, edited by Richard Morris, 6 vols. London: Pāli Text Society, 1955–76.

AV: **Abhidharmavibhāṣā* ascribed to Kātyāyanīputra. *Apitan piposha lun* (阿毘曇毘婆沙論), trans. Buddhavarman and Daotai (道泰), T1546.

BBh: *Bodhisattvabhūmi: A Statement of Whole Course of the Bodhisattva (Being Fifteenth Section of Yogācārabhūmi)*, edited by Unrai Wogihara. Tokyo: Sankibo Buddhist Book Store, 1971.

gCig du bral gyi rnam bzhag of A lag sha ngag dbang bstan dar. Tibetan text in Tillemans (1999: 258–65); English translation by Tillemans and Lopez in Tillemans (1999: 249–58).

D: The Derge edition of Tibetan Tripiṭaka.

JDZL: *Jue ding zang lun* (決定藏論), trans. Paramārtha, T1584.

Jushe lun ji (俱舍論記) of Puguang (普光), T1821.

Jushe lun shu (俱舍論疏) of Fabao (法寶), T1822.

JP: **Janakaparamopadeśa* of Harivarman. *Cheng shi lun* (成實論), trans. Kumārajīva, T1646.

Kathāvatthu ascribed to Tissa Moggaliputta. *The Kathā-vatthu*, edited by A. C. Taylor. London: Pāli Text Society, 1894–97.

Kathāvatthu-aṭṭhakathā of Buddhaghosa. *Kathāvatthuppakaraṇa-aṭṭhakathā*, edited by N. A. Jayawickrama. London: Pāli Text Society, 1979.

Limenlun shuji (理門論述記) of Shentai (神泰), T1839.

Madhyama Āgama. *Zhong ahan jing* (中阿含經), trans. Saṃghadeva, T26.

Majjhima Nikāya. *The Majjhima-Nikāya*, edited by V. Trenchner, R. Chalmers, and C. A. F. Rhys Davids, 4 vols. London: Pali Text Society, [1888–1925] 1977–93.

MV: *Mahāvibhāṣa* ascribed to 500 arhats. *Apidamo da piposha lun* (阿毘達磨大毘婆沙論), trans. Xuanzang (玄奘), T1545.

MSṬ: **Mahāyānasaṃgrahatīka* of Asvabhāva. *She dacheng lun shi* (攝大乘論釋), Chinese trans. Xuanzang, T1598; *Theg pa chen po bsdus pa'i bshad sbyar*, Tibetan trans. Jinamitra, Sīlendrabodhi, and Ye shes sde, P5552.

NA: **Nyāyānusāra* of Saṃghabhadra. *Apidamo shun zhengli lun* (阿毘達磨順正理論), trans. Xuanzang, T1562.

Nyāyamukha of Dignāga. *Yinming zhengli men lun* 因明正理門論, trans. Xuanzang, T1628.

Nyāyapraveśa of Śaṅkarasvāmin. *The Nyāyapraveśa*, edited by A. B. Dhruva, Part I, Sanskrit Text with Commentaries. Baroda: Oriental Institute, 1968.

P: The Peking edition of Tibetan Tripiṭaka.

Pramāṇasamuccayavṛtti of Dignāga. *Tshad ma kun las btus pa'i 'grel pa*, trans. Kanakavarman and Dad pa'i shes rab, P5702.

Pramāṇasamuccayavṛtti of Dignāga. *Tshad ma kun las btus pa'i 'grel pa*, trans. Vasudhararakṣita and Seng rgyal, P5701; D4204.

Pramāṇavārttika-svavṛtti of Dharmakīrti, edited by R. Gnoli. Roma, 1960.

PV: *Pramāṇavṛttika*, see Miyasaka (1971–72).

PVV: *The Pramāṇavṛttikam of Ācārya Dharmakīrti with the Commentaries, Svopajñavṛtti of the Author and Pramāṇavṛttikavṛtti of Manorathanandin*, edited by R. Ch. Pandeya. Delhi: Motilal Banarsidass, 1989.

Śāriputrābhidharma. Shelifu apitan (舍利弗阿毘曇), trans. Dharmayaśas and Dharmagupta, T1548.

Samayabhedoparacanacakra of Vasumitra. *Yibu zonglun lun* (異部宗輪論), Chinese trans. Xuanzang, T2031; *gZhung lugs kyi bye brag bkod pa'i 'khor lo*, Tibetan trans. Dharmākara and Bzang skyong, P5639.

Saṃyukta Āgama. Za ahan jing (雜阿含經), trans. Guṇabhadra, T99.

Saṃyutta Nikāya. The Saṃyutta-Nikāya, edited by L. Feer, 6 vols. London: Pāli Text Society, [1884–1904] 1975–91.

Ślokavārttika of Kumārila. *Ślokavārttikavyākhyā (Tātparyaṭīkā) of Bhaṭṭombeka*, edited by S. K. Rāmanātha Śāstri, Madras University Sanskrit Series, no. 13. Madras, 1940.

T: CBETA *Chinese Electronic Tripiṭaka: Taishō Edition Vols 1–55, 85*. Available online: http://cbetaonline.dila.edu.tw (accessed January 31, 2019).

Tattvasaṃgrahapañjikā of Kamalaśīla. *Tattvasaṅgraha of ācārya Shāntarakṣita with the commentary "Pañjikā" of Shrī Kamalashīla*, edited by S. Dwarikadas Shastri, 2 vols. Varanasi: Bauddha Bharati Series 1, [1968] 1981.

Vijñānakāya of Devaśarman. *Apidamo shi shen zu lun* (阿毘達磨識身足論), trans. Xuanzang, T1539.

X: *Xuzangjing* (卍續藏經). Available online: http://cbetaonline.dila.edu.tw (accessed January 31, 2019).

YBh: *Yogācārabhūmi*, attributed to Maitreyanātha or Asaṅga.

YBhc: *Yujia shidi lun* (瑜伽師地論), Chinese translation of *Yogācārabhūmi* by Xuanzang, T1579.

YBhs: *The Yogācārabhūmi of Ācārya Asaṅga: The Sanskrit Text Compared with the Tibetan Version*, edited by Vidhushekhara Bhattacharya. Calcutta: University of Calcutta, 1957.

YBht: *rNal 'byor spyod pa'i sa rnam par gtan la dbab pa bsdu ba*, Tibetan translation of the *Viniścayasaṃgrahaṇī* section of *Yogācārabhūmi* by Prajñāvarman, Surendrabodhi, and Ye shes sde, D4038.

Yibu zonglun lun shuji (異部宗輪論述記) of Kuiji (窺基), X844.

Yinming ru zhengli lun yi zuanyao (因明入正理論義纂要) of Huizhao (慧沼), T1842.

Yinming ru zhengli lunshu (因明入正理論疏) of Kuiji, T1840.

Secondary Sources

Abe, Masao (1985), "Non-being and *Mu*—the Metaphysical Nature of Negativity in the East and the West," in *Zen and Western Thought*, edited by William R. LaFleur, 128–30. London: Macmillan.

Benoist, Jocelyn (2001), "La théorie phénoménologique de la négation, entre acte et sens." *Revue de Métaphysique et de Morale* 2: 21–35.

Carnap, Rudolf (1931), "Überwindung der Metaphysik durch logische Analyse der Sprache." *Erkenntnis* 2: 219–41.

Chakrabarti, Arindam (1997), *Denying Existence*. Dordrecht: Kluwer Academic Publishers.

Chu, Junjie (2004), "A Study of Sataimira in Dignāga's Definition of Pseudo-Perception (PS 1.7cd–8ab)." *Wiener Zeitschrift für die Kunde Südasiens* 48: 113–49.

Cox, Collett (1988), "On the Possibility of a Nonexistent Object of Consciousness: Sarvāstivādin and Dārṣṭāntika Theories." *Journal of the International Association of Buddhist Studies* 11 (1): 31–87.

Cox, Collett (1995), *Disputed Dharmas—Early Buddhist Theories on Existence—An Annotated Translation of the Section on Factors Dissociated from Thought from Saṅghabhadra's Nyāyānusāra*, Studia Philologica Buddhica, Monograph Series 11, Tokyo.

Crane, Tim (2013), *The Objects of Thought*. Oxford and New York: Oxford University Press.

Dhammajoti, K. L. (2007a), *Abhidharma Doctrine and Controversy on Perception*. Hong Kong: Centre of Buddhist Studies, University of Hong Kong.

Dhammajoti, K. L. (2007b), *Sarvāstivāda Abhidharma*. Hong Kong: Centre of Buddhist Studies, University of Hong Kong.

Edgerton, Franklin, ed. and trans. (1986), *Mīmāṃsānyāyaprakāśa*. Delhi: Sri Satguru Publications.

Franco, Eli (2004), "Xuanzang's Proof of Idealism (*Vijñaptimātratā*)." *Hōrin* 11: 199–211.

Frankenhauser, Uwe (1996), *Die Einführung der buddhistischen Logik in China*. Wiesbaden: Harrassowitz Verlag.

Funayama, Toru (1991), "On *Āśrayāsiddha*." *Journal of Indian and Buddhist Studies* 39 (2): 1027–1.

Graham, A. C. (1965), "'Being' in Linguistics and Philosophy: A Preliminary Inquiry." *Foundations of Language* 1 (3): 223–31.

Guha, Nirmalya (2013), "No Black Scorpion Is Falling: An Onto-Epistemic Analysis of Absence." *Journal of Indian Philosophy* 41: 111–31.

Harbsmeier, Christoph (1998), *Science and Civilisation in China Volume 7 Part I: Language and Logic*. Cambridge: Cambridge University Press.

Harvey, Charles W. and Jaakko Hintikka (1991), "Modalization and Modalities," in *Phenomenology and the Formal Sciences*, edited by Th. M. Seebohm, Thomas M. Seebohm, Dagfinn Føllesdal, and J. N. Mohanty. Dordrecht: Kluwer.

Heidegger, Martin (1963), *Sein und Zeit*. Tübingen: Max Niemeyer Verlag.

Heidegger, Martin (1978), "Was ist Metaphysik?" *Wegmarken*, GA 9, Frankfurt am Main: Vittorio Klostermann.

Heidegger, Martin (1990), *Metaphysische Anfangsgründe der Logik im Ausgang von Leibniz*, GA 26, Frankfurt am Main: V. Klostermann.

Heidegger, Martin (1997), *Besinnung*, GA 66, Frankfurt am Main: V. Klostermann.

Heidegger, Martin (1998), *Pathmarks*, edited by William McNeill. Cambridge: Cambridge University Press.

Heidegger, Martin (1999), *Contributions to Philosophy (from Enowning)*, translated by Parvis Emad and Kenneth Maly. Bloomington: Indiana University Press.

Horn, Laurence R. (1989), *A Natural History of Negation*. Chicago: University of Chicago Press.

Husserl, Edmund (1973), *Experience and Judgment: Investigations in a Genealogy of Logic*, translated by J. S. Churchill and K. Ameriks. London: Routledge & Kegan Paul.

Husserl, Edmund (2001), *Analyses Concerning Passive and Active Synthesis: Lectures on Transcendental Logic*, translated by Anthony J. Steinbock. Dordrecht: Kluwer.

Kajiyama, Yuichi (1973), "Three Kinds of Affirmation and Two Kinds of Negation in Buddhist Philosophy." *Wiener Zeitschrift für die Kunde Südasiens* 17: 161–75.

Kant, Immanuel (1956), *Kritik der reinen Vernunft*. Hamburg: Verlag von Felix Meiner.

Katō, Junshō (加藤純章) (1989), *Kyōryōbu no kenkyū* (經量部の研究). Tokyo: Shunjūsha.

Katsura, Shoryu (桂紹隆) (1981), "Immyō shōri mon ron kenkyū (IV)" (因明正理門論研究（四）). *Hiroshima Daigaku Bungakubu kiyō* (広島大学文学部紀要) 41: 62–82.

Katsura, Shoryu (1992), "Dignāga and Dharmakīrti on *adarśanamātra* and *anupalabdhi*." *Asiatische Studien* 46 (1): 222–31.

Kellner, Birgit (1997a), *Nichts bleibt nichts. Die buddhistische Zurückweisung von Kumārilas abhāvapramāṇa. Übersetzung und Interpretation von Śāntarakṣitas Tattvasaṃgraha vv. 1647–1690 mit Kamalaśīlas Tattvasaṃgrahapañjikā sowie Ansätze und Arbeitshypothesen zur Geschichte negativer Erkenntnis in der indischen Philosophie*, Wiener Studien zur Tibetologie und Buddhismuskunde 39, Wien.

Kellner, Birgit (1997b), "Non-cognition (*Anupalabdhi*)—Perception or Inference? The Views of Dharmottara and Jñānaśrīmitra." *Tetsugaku* 49: 121–34.

Kellner, Birgit (1999), "Levels of (Im)perceptibility: Dharmottara on the *dṛśya* in *Dṛśyānupalabdhi*," in *Dharmakīrti's Thought and Its Impact on Indian and Tibetan Philosophy*, Proceedings of the Third International Dharmakīrti Conference, Hiroshima, November 4–6, 1997, 193–208, Wien.

Kellner, Birgit (2001), "Negation—Failure or Success? Remarks on an Allegedly Characteristic Trait of Dharmakīrti's *Anupalabdhi*-Theory." *Journal of Indian Philosophy* 29: 495–517.

Kellner, Birgit (2003), "Integrating Negative Knowledge into *Pramāṇa* Theory: The Development of the *Dṛśyānupalabdhi* in Dharmakīrti's Earlier Works." *Journal of Indian Philosophy* 31: 121–59.

Kitagawa, Hidenori (北川秀則) (1965), *Indo koten ronrigaku no kenkyū; Jinna (Dignāga) no taikei* (インド古典論理学の研究; 陳那 (Dignāga) の体系). Tokyo: Suzuki Gakujutsu Zaidan.

Kobusch, Theo (1984), "Nichts, Nichtseiendes," in *Historisches Wörterbuch der Philosophie*, Band 6, 813–19. Basel and Stuttgart: Schwabe & Co AG Verlag.

Kriegel, Uriah (2008), "The Dispensability of (Merely) Intentional Objects." *Philosophical Studies* 141: 79–95.

Kritzer, Robert (2005), *Vasubandhu and the* Yogācārabhūmi: *Yogācāra Elements in the* Abhidharmakośabhāṣya. Tokyo: International Institute for Buddhist Studies of the International College for Postgraduate Buddhist Studies.

Krysztofiak, Wojciech (1992), "Phenomenology, Possible Worlds and Negation." *Husserl Studies* 8: 205–20.

Kwan, Siu Tong (2007), "The Semantic Problem of the Non-existent Object in Abhidharma Buddhism." *Journal of Buddhist Studies* 5: 243–58.

Kwan, Tze-wan (1982), *Die hermeneutische Phänomenologie und das tautologische Denken Heideggers*. Bonn: Bouvier Verlag Herbert Grundmann.

La Vallée Poussin, Louis de (1928–29), *Vijñaptimātratāsiddhi: La Siddhi de Huian-Tsang*, 2 vols. Paris: Librairie Orientaliste Paul Geuthner.

La Vallée Poussin, Louis de (1936–37), "Documents d'abhidharma: la controverse du temps." *Mélanges chinois et bouddhiques* 5: 25–128.

La Vallée Poussin, Louis de (1971), *L'Abhidharmakośa de Vasubandhu*. Tome IV, Institut Belge des Hautes Études Chinoises.

Li, Xuezhu (李学竹) (2013), "*Abhidharmadīpa* no jobun nitsuite." (*Abhidharmadīpa* の序文について), *Indogaku Bukkyōgaku Kenkyū* 65 (1): 379–3.

Lin, Chen-Kuo (林鎮國) (1999), *Kongxing yu xiandaixing: cong Jingdu xuepai, xinrujia dao duoyin de fojiao quanshixue* (空性與現代性: 從京都學派, 新儒家到多音的佛教詮釋學). Taipei: Lixu wenhua shiye youxian gongsi.

Lin, Chien-Te (林建德) (2007), "Laozi yu Zhonglun zhi zhexue bijiao" (老子與中論之哲學比較), PhD diss., National Taiwan University.

Liu, Xiaogan (劉笑敢) (1997), *Lao Zi* (老子). Taipei: Dongda tushu gongsi.

Lohmar, Dieter (1992), "Beiträge zu einer phänomenologischen Theorie des negativen Urteils." *Husserl Studies* 8: 173–204.

Lü, Cheng (呂澂) (1991), *Lü Cheng foxue lunzhu xuanji* (呂澂佛學論著選集). Jinan: Qi Lu shushe.

Luo, Yin (羅因) (2003), *"Kong," "you" yu "you," "wu": xuanxue yu borexue jiaohui wenti zhi yanjiu* (「空」・「有」與「有」・「無」: 玄学與般若學交會問題之研究). Taipei: Guoli taiwan daxue chuban weiyuanhui.

Lusthaus, Dan (2002), *Buddhist Phenomenology*. New York and London: RoutledgeCurzon.

Matilal, Bimal K. (1968), *The Navya-Nyāya Doctrine of Negation*. Cambridge, MA: Harvard University Press.

Matilal, Bimal K. (1985), *Logic, Language & Reality: Indian Philosophy and Contemporary Issues*. Delhi: Motilal Banarsidass.

May, Reinhard (1996), *Heidegger's Hidden Sources: East-Asian Influences on His Work*, translated with a complementary essay by Graham Parkes. London: Routledge.

McDermott, A. C. S. (1970), "Empty Subject Terms in Late Buddhist Logic." *Journal of Indian Philosophy* 1: 22–9.

Miyasaka, Yūshō (1971–72), "Pramāṇavārttika-kārikā (Sanskrit and Tibetan)." *Acta Indologica* 2: 1–206.

Miyashita, Seiki (宮下晴輝) (1986), "Kusharon ni okeru hon mu kon u ron no haikei: Shōgi kūsho kyō no kaishaku o megutte" (『倶舎論』における本無今有論の背景: 『勝義空性経』の解釈をめぐって). *Bukkyōgaku seminā* (仏教学セミナー) 44: 7–37.

Nagao, Gajin (1991), *Mādhyamika and Yogācāra: A Study of Mahāyāna Philosophies*, edited, collated, and translated by L. S. Kawamura in collaboration with G. M. Nagao. Albany: State University of New York Press.

Odani, Nobuchiyo (小谷信千代) and Honjō Yoshifumi (本庄良文) (2007), *Kusharon no genten kenkyū: zuiminbon* (倶舎論の原典研究: 随眠品). Tokyo: Daizō Shuppan.

Ono, Motoi, Oda Jun'ichi, Takashima Jun (1996), *KWIC Index to the Sanskrit Texts of Dharmakīrti*, Lexicological Studies 8. Tokyo: Tokyo University of Foreign Studies.

Pang, Pu (龐樸) (1999), "Shuo 'wu'" (說「無」), in *Dangdai xuezhe zixuan wenku Pang Pu juan* (當代學者自選文庫龐樸卷), 348–63. Hefei: Anhui jiaoyu chubanshe.

Perszyk, Kenneth J. (1984), "The Nyāya and Russell on Empty Terms." *Philosophy East and West* 34 (2): 131–46.

Priest, Graham (2009), "Not to Be," in *The Routledge Companion to Metaphysics*, edited by Robin Le Poidevin, Peter Simons, Andrew McGonigal, and Ross P. Cameron, 234–45. London and New York: Routledge.

Priest, Graham (2016), *Towards Non-being: The Logic and Metaphysics of Intentionality*. Oxford and New York: Oxford University Press.

Russell, Bertrand (1994), "On Denoting [1905]," in *The Collected Papers of Bertrand Russell*, Volume 4: "Foundations of Logic 1903–05," 414–27. London and New York: Routledge.

Sakamoto, Yukio (坂本幸男) (1981), *Abidatsuma no kenkyū* (阿毘達磨の研究). Tokyo: Daito Shuppansha.

Searle, John R. (1969), *Speech Acts: An Essay in the Philosophy of Language*. London: Cambridge University Press.

Shaw, J. L. (1974), "Empty Terms: The Nyāya and the Buddhists." *Journal of Indian Philosophy* 2: 332–43.

Shen, Jianying (沈劍英) (2002), *Yinming xue yanjiu*(因明學研究). Shanghai: Dongfang chuban zhongxin.

Shwe Zan Aung and Rhys Davids ([1915] 1969), *Points of Controversy; or, Subjects of Discourse/Being a Translation of the Kathā-vatthu from the Abhidhammapiṭaka*. London: Pub. for the Pali Text Society by Luzac & Co.

Siderits, Mark (1991), *Indian Philosophy of Language: Studies in Selected Issues.* Dordrecht: Kluwer Academic Publishers.

Sorensen, Roy (2017), "Nothingness," in *Stanford Encyclopedia of Philosophy*. Available online: http://plato.stanford.edu/entries/nothingness/ (accessed January 31, 2019).

Stambaugh, Joan (trans.) (1996), *Being and Time: A Translation of Sein und Zeit.* Albany: State University of New York Press.

Steinkellner, Ernst (1966), "Bemerkungen zu Īśvarasenas Lehre vom Grund." *Wiener Zeitschrift für die Kunde Süd- und Ostasiens* 10: 73–85.

Steinkellner, Ernst (1992), "Lamotte and the Concept of Anupalabdhi." *Asiatische Studien* 46 (1): 398–410.

Taber, John (2001), "Much Ado about Nothing: Kumārila, Śāntarakṣita, and Dharmakīrti on the Cognition of Non-being." *Journal of the American Oriental Society* 121 (1): 72–88.

Tillemans, Tom J. (1999), *Scripture, Logic, Language: Essays on Dharmakīrti and His Tibetan Successors*. Boston: Wisdom Publications.

Tosaki, Hiromasa (戸崎宏正) (1979), *Bukkyō ninshikiron no kenkyū* (仏教認識論の研究), vol. 1. Tokyo: Daito Shuppansha.

Tsukamoto, Keishō (塚本啓祥), Matsunaga Yūkei (松長有慶), and Isoda Hirofumi (磯田熙文) (1990), *Bongo butten no kenkyū* (梵語仏典の研究), vol. 3. Kyoto: Heirakuji Shoten.

Wang, Zhongjiang (王中江) (2001), *Daojia xingershangxue* (道家形而上学). Shanghai: Shanghai wenhua chubanshe.

Watanabe, Toshikazu (渡辺俊和) (2002), ("Dharmakīrti" の非認識論—相反関係を中心に). *Nanto Bukkyō* 81: 54–80.

Wirtz, Markus (2006), *Geschichten des Nichts: Hegel, Nietzsche, Heidegger und das Problem der philosophischen Pluralität*. Freiburg, München: Verlag Karl Alber.

Yaita, Hideomi (矢板秀臣) (1984), "Hōshō no 'hininshiki'" (法称の「非認識」), in *Chūgoku no shūkyō shisō to kagaku. Makyo Ryōkai-hakase Jujukinenronshū* (中国の宗教・思想と科学： 牧尾良海博士頌寿記念論集), 34–45. Tokyo.

Yaita, Hideomi (1985a), "On Anupalabdhi, Annotated Translation of Dharmakīrti's Pramāṇa-vārttika-svavṛtti (I)." *Taishōdaigaku Daigakuin Kenkyūronshū* 9: 216–199.

Yaita, Hideomi (1985b), "On Anupalabdhi, Annotated Translation of Dharmakīrti's Pramāṇa-vārttika-svavṛtti (II)." *Chizan Gakuhō* 34: 1–14.

Yao, Zhihua (2005), *The Buddhist Theory of Self-Cognition*. London and New York: Routledge.

Yao, Zhihua (2006), "A Note on Asvabhāva and Dignāga." *Journal of Buddhist Studies* 4: 251–8.

Yoshimoto, Shingyō (吉元信行) (1982), *Abidaruma shisō* (アビダルマ思想). Kyoto: Hōzōkan.

Zhao, Weiwei (趙偉偉) (2007), "Laozi de wu yu Zhonglun de kong zhi yitong" (老子的無與中論的空之異同). *Zhongguo zhexue yu wenhua* (中國哲學與文化) 2: 324–41.

INDEX

A lag sha ngag dbang bstan dar 120–2
Abe, M. 152
Abhidharma 14, 18, 20, 22, 25, 37, 48, 51, 150
absolute nonexistence 4, 64, 79, 81–3, 87–8, 104, 109
absolute nothing 8–9, 141, 147, 154
adarśanamātra 5, 22, 95, 99, 102, 109
affirmative judgments 168n3
ālambana-pratyaya 3, 69, 86
ālaya-vijñāna 15
all-encompassing spheres 39–40, 43–4, 46
analogy 94, 132
Andhaka 17–21, 27, 43–4, 46
Angst 142–3, 145–6
antirealism 46
anupalabdhi 5, 22, 94–5, 99, 101–5, 109, 118, 132
anuśaya 13–19, 23, 26–7, 29–30, 66. *See also* latent defilements
anyonyābhāva 4, 64, 79, 109, 149. *See also* mutual nonexistence
apoha 95, 111, 113, 118
arhat 15, 21, 27
arthakriyā 3, 119. *See also* causal efficacy
Asaṅga 96, 103–6, 109
Asvabhāva 93, 105–7, 109–10, 169n21
ātman 56, 71
atoms 80–1, 87, 107
atyantābhāva 4, 64, 79, 81, 104, 109, 149. *See also* absolute nonexistence, absolute nothing
Augustine 142

Befindlichkeit 142
Benoist, J. 134
bodily feeling 31, 45
Buddhaghosa 17, 20, 23, 44, 46
buddhi 33, 38, 47, 55, 82

caitta 20, 27, 57. *See also* mental activities
Carnap, R. 142
causal efficacy 3, 119
Chakrabarti, A. 6
Chan 107, 144
Chang'an 107
Chu, J. 97
Ci'en 110
conceptual construction 31–2, 35, 97, 108, 118–19, 152
conceptual subjects 7, 113, 117–18, 120, 126, 128
conjunction 30–1, 45, 66
Cox, C. 18, 22, 36, 65, 88
Crane, T. 4

Daoism 8–9, 142–4, 147, 153, 155
Dasein 142–6
Devaśarman 25–6
Dhammajoti 65, 69
dharmadhātu 152
Dharmaguptaka 14, 16, 18, 22, 25–8, 33, 37, 39, 46, 88
dharmakāya 104–5
Dharmakīrti 5–6, 79, 93–5, 97, 99–107, 109–11, 113, 115, 117–20, 126, 129, 132–4, 136, 139–40, 168n1
Dharmapāla 93, 98, 107, 109, 127
Dharmatrāta 31–2
dhvaṃsa 4, 64, 79, 109, 149. *See also* posterior nonexistence
Dignāga 5, 94–7, 100, 102–3, 106, 109, 111–18, 120–1, 125–6
double moon 35, 130

dream-images 34–5
Dunhuang 108, 110
Dunnyun 57–8, 107

Ekavyavahārika 14, 16, 26
emptiness 6, 9, 112, 117, 120, 142, 149–53, 172n14
enmity 15, 17
Ereignis 145

feiliang 93, 96–9, 101, 105–10, 168n6
fire-wheel 32–4
Furcht 143

Gandharva 32–3
ghosts 5, 102, 132, 140
Graham, A. 73
Greek 4, 83, 89

Harivarman 29, 35–7, 39–41, 43, 45–6, 69, 71, 83
Hegel, G. 143–6, 148
Heidegger, M. 8–9, 142–6, 148–9, 153–5
Horn, L. 57, 122
Huijing 58
Huizhao 114, 119–21
Husserl, E. 79, 129, 133–40

illocutionary negation 130–2
imaginary entity (*ens imaginarium*) 173n3
impermanence 6, 37, 56–9, 64, 67, 75, 81, 87, 108, 112
implicative negation 7, 120–2
indriya 19, 71
intentionality 63–4, 137
Īśvara 83
Īśvarasena 5, 93, 95–6, 99–102, 106–7, 109–10, 131–2, 134, 136, 168n1

Jambudvīpa 41
janaka-pratyaya 2, 3, 69, 86
Jinaputra 93, 106, 109–10
Jñānaśrīmitra 171n13
jñeyatva 1–3, 80

Kamalaśīla 71–2, 114, 120
Kant, I. 142, 146
karma 4, 68, 74, 108
Kāśyapīya 4, 68
Katō, J. 69
Katsura, S. 95, 118
Kaukkuṭika 14, 16, 26
Kellner, B. 94–5, 99, 132
Kierkegaard, S. 143
Krysztofiak, W. 134–5, 137, 139
Kuiji 15, 52, 60–1, 97–8, 107, 109–10, 122, 125–6
Kumāralāta 69
Kumārila 5, 93–4, 104, 109, 131–2, 134, 136, 168n1

La Vallée Poussin, L. 65, 68
Lacan, J. 19, 27
Lao Zi 147–9
latent defilements 13, 16–19, 23, 27–9, 45, 66
Leibniz, G. 1, 141, 153–4
light 43, 84
Lohmar, D. 138
Lokottaravāda 14, 16, 26

Madhyamaka 9, 117, 120, 149–53
magical creations 34, 45
Mahīśāsaka 14–16, 18, 22, 25–6, 33, 37, 88
Maitreyanātha 96
manifested defilements 14–16, 27, 30
Matilal, B. 111, 114, 120, 130
Maudgalyāyana 25–6
McDermott, A. 111
meditation 15, 25, 35, 37–42, 46, 84
Meinong, A. 2–3, 24, 117–19, 124, 128–9, 140
mental activities 14–16, 18, 20, 22, 27, 57
mental feeling 31–2, 45
Mīmāṃsaka 5, 93–4, 123, 131, 138, 149
mindless meditation 15–16, 27
mirage 32–4, 45
mirror-images 33
Miyasaka, Y. 97
Moists 9, 154
molecule (*aṇu*) 107, 170n25
mutual nonexistence 4, 64, 79, 109, 169n18

Nagao, G. 152
Nāgārjuna 103, 150–1
Naiyāyika 5, 130–32, 134, 136, 138–9, 149
Nālandā 127
negation 5–7, 56–7, 96, 100, 120–2, 130–40, 145–6, 151, 173n4
negative nothing 8, 9, 141, 146–8, 150–1, 153
Neo-Confucian 147
Nichts 142–3
nihil negativum 146–7. *See also* negative nothing
nihil originarium 146–7. *See also* original nothing
nihil privativum 146–7. *See also* privative nothing
nihilism 61–2, 149
nirvāṇa 17, 19, 57, 71, 85–6, 103, 105
Noch-nichtsein 173n4
nominal existence 36, 83, 87
non-implicative negation 7, 112, 120–2
no-self 6, 55–9, 64, 112, 149
nothing altogether 38, 82
Nyāya 60, 94–5, 97–8, 102, 111–12, 115, 171n13

objectless presentations 129
optical illusions 33, 45
ordinary person 15–6, 18, 27
original nothing 8–9, 141, 146–9, 151–4
other-emptiness (*gzhan stong*) 152

pan-fictionalism 111, 119–20, 123, 171n13
Pang, P. 147
paramāṇu 107. *See also* atoms
Paramārtha 48–9, 61
Parmenides 1, 4, 8–10, 63, 83, 89, 141, 143, 146, 153–4
particulars 39, 42, 58–61, 108–9, 118
paryavasthāna 14–16, 27, 30, 67. *See also* manifested defilements
paryudāsa 7, 120–1. *See also* implicative negation
Perszyk, K. 111
perversion 42–4
pillar 34, 45, 76
Plato 10, 141–3, 146, 154
posterior nonexistence 4, 64, 73, 79, 81, 87, 109, 169n18
pradhāna 102–3, 112, 116. *See also* primordial matter
prāgabhāva 4, 64, 78–9, 109, 149. *See also* prior nonexistence
Prajñākaragupta 113, 115, 120
pramāṇa, sixfold 168n2
prasajya-pratiṣedha 7, 120–1. *See also* non-implicative negation
presumption 94, 132
Priest, G. 4, 89, 124
primordial matter 102–3, 112–13, 115–16, 118–19, 121, 123–5
prior nonexistence 4, 64, 109, 169n18
privative nothing 8–9, 141, 146–8, 150–1, 153
propositional attitude 7, 112–14, 116, 123, 125–7
propositional negation 130–2, 134
pseudo-inference 97–8, 107, 109
pseudo-perception 97–8, 107, 109, 138
Pubbaseliya 20–1, 27
pudgala 31, 62
puruṣa 62, 116

rational entity (*ens rationis*) 173n3
Ratnakīrti 171n13
realism 46, 60, 117, 123, 127, 149
reflexive awareness 21, 27, 33
resolving attention 39, 40, 42
Russell, B. 6, 8, 111, 114, 117, 119, 127, 129

Sakamoto, Y. 22, 65
Śākya mchog ldan 121
sāmānyalakṣaṇa 39, 56, 58, 61, 118. *See also* universals
samāpatti 15, 43
Saṃghabhadra 29, 38–40, 42–3, 46, 66, 69–72, 76–7, 79–80, 82, 84–5, 89
Saṃmatīya 16, 27
saṃyoga 30–1, 66. *See also* conjunction
Śaṅkarasvāmin 97–8, 109
Sāṅkhya 112–13, 115, 123–5

Śāntarakṣita 94
Sautrāntika 3, 10, 13, 23, 26, 28, 32–3, 39, 45, 49, 60, 65–6, 68–9, 88, 149
Schelling, F. 143, 146
Searle, J. 130
Sein 2, 117
self-emptiness (*rang stong*) 152
shadow 33–4, 45, 146
Shaw, J. 111
Shentai 115–16, 125
sky-flower 52, 83
snake 34, 45
son of a barren woman 4, 9, 55, 57, 64, 81, 151, 154
Sosein 2, 117
space 36, 40, 103–4, 141, 147
square-circle 151, 154
Śrīlāta 69
Steinkellner, E. 93, 95, 103
Sthaviravāda 14, 27
śūnyatā 6, 74, 81, 103, 112, 142. *See also* emptiness
svalakṣaṇa 39, 58, 118. *See also* particulars
svasaṃvedana 13, 98

Tankuang 108–10
tathatā 152
theory of descriptions 8, 111, 114, 117, 127
Theravādin 17, 19, 23–4, 27–8, 43, 46
thirteenth sense-sphere 81–4, 87–8
Tillemans, T. 113–15, 118–21, 126
Tosaki, H. 100
Tsong kha pa 114, 120–2

Uddyotakara 130
universals 4, 39, 56, 58–61, 64, 108–9, 118
unmanifested matter 31–2, 163n31
Uttarāpathaka 17, 23–6, 28, 39, 88

vaipulya 56, 59, 61, 162n21
Vaiśeṣika 1, 4, 63, 71, 149
vastu 30–1
Vasumitra 14, 25
verbal testimony 94, 132
Vetulyaka 162n21
Vibhajyavādin 13, 14, 25–6, 68, 77, 88

Wang Bi 148
Watanabe, T. 132
Wŏnch'ŭk 110
wondrous being 152

Ximing 110
Xuan School 147–8
Xuanzang 48–9, 58, 74, 96, 126

Yaita, H. 95, 99
Yao, Z. 13, 21
Yaśomitra 70–1
yogic perception 59
yogic practitioner 40, 55
Yoshimoto, S. 65

www.ingramcontent.com/pod-product-compliance
Lightning Source LLC
Chambersburg PA
CBHW052045300426
44117CB00012B/1988
9781350273108